LITTLE WOMEN

BY
L.M.ALCOTT

SINCE *LITTLE WOMEN* WAS first published more than 150 years ago, Louisa May Alcott's classic novel has never gone out of print.

Little Women

EDITORIAL DIRECTOR Kostya Kennedy
DIRECTOR OF PHOTOGRAPHY Christina Lieberman
ART DIRECTOR Lan Yin Bachelis
WRITER Gina McIntyre
COPY CHIEF Parlan McGaw
COPY EDITOR Joel Van Liew
PICTURE EDITORS Rachel Hatch, Michelle Molloy
WRITER-REPORTER Emily Joshu
PHOTO ASSISTANT Steph Durante
PRODUCTION DESIGN Sandra Jurevics
PREMEDIA TRAFFICKING SUPERVISOR Sarah Schuster
COLOR QUALITY ANALYST Pamela Powers

MEREDITH SPECIAL INTEREST MEDIA
VICE PRESIDENT & GROUP PUBLISHER Scott Mortimer
VICE PRESIDENT, GROUP EDITORIAL DIRECTOR Stephen Orr
VICE PRESIDENT, MARKETING Jeremy Biloon
EXECUTIVE ACCOUNT DIRECTOR Doug Stark
DIRECTOR, BRAND MARKETING Jean Kennedy
ASSOCIATE DIRECTOR, BRAND MARKETING Bryan Christian
SENIOR BRAND MANAGER Katherine Barnet

EDITORIAL DIRECTOR Kostya Kennedy
CREATIVE DIRECTOR Gary Stewart
DIRECTOR OF PHOTOGRAPHY Christina Lieberman
EDITORIAL OPERATIONS DIRECTOR Jamie Roth Major
MANAGER, EDITORIAL OPERATIONS Gina Scauzillo

SPECIAL THANKS Brad Beatson, Melissa Frankenberry, Samantha Lebofsky, Kate Roncinske, Laura Villano

MEREDITH NATIONAL MEDIA GROUP
PRESIDENT, MEREDITH MAGAZINES Doug Olson
PRESIDENT, CONSUMER PRODUCTS Tom Witschi
PRESIDENT, CHIEF DIGITAL OFFICER Catherine Levene
CHIEF REVENUE OFFICER Michael Brownstein
CHIEF MARKETING & DATA OFFICER Alysia Borsa
MARKETING & INTEGRATED COMMUNICATIONS Nancy Weber

SENIOR VICE PRESIDENTS
CONSUMER REVENUE Andy Wilson
CORPORATE SALES Brian Kightlinger
DIRECT MEDIA Patti Follo
RESEARCH SOLUTIONS Britta Cleveland
STRATEGIC SOURCING, NEWSSTAND, PRODUCTION Chuck Howell
DIGITAL SALES Marla Newman
THE FOUNDRY Matt Petersen
PRODUCT & TECHNOLOGY Justin Law

VICE PRESIDENTS
FINANCE Chris Susil
BUSINESS PLANNING & ANALYSIS Rob Silverstone
CONSUMER MARKETING Steve Crowe
BRAND LICENSING Steve Grune
CORPORATE COMMUNICATIONS Jill Davison

VICE PRESIDENT, GROUP EDITORIAL DIRECTOR Stephen Orr
DIRECTOR, EDITORIAL OPERATIONS & FINANCE Greg Kayko

MEREDITH CORPORATION
PRESIDENT & CHIEF EXECUTIVE OFFICER Tom Harty
CHIEF FINANCIAL OFFICER Joseph Ceryanec
CHIEF DEVELOPMENT OFFICER John Zieser
CHIEF STRATEGY OFFICER Daphne Kwon
PRESIDENT, MEREDITH LOCAL MEDIA GROUP Patrick McCreery
SENIOR VICE PRESIDENT, HUMAN RESOURCES Dina Nathanson

CHAIRMAN Stephen M. Lacy
VICE CHAIRMAN Mell Meredith Frazier

Copyright © 2020 Meredith Corporation

225 Liberty Street • New York, NY 10281

All rights reserved. No part of this book may be reproduced in any form or by any electronic or mechanical means, including information storage and retrieval systems, without permission in writing from the publisher, except by a reviewer, who may quote brief passages in a review.

For syndication requests or international licensing requests or reprint and reuse permission, e-mail syndication@meredith.com.

PRINTED IN THE USA

LIFE is a registered trademark, registered in the U.S. and other countries.

Special thanks to Maria Powers, assistant to the executive director of Louisa May Alcott's Orchard House, for sharing her resources and deep knowledge of Louisa May Alcott's life and history.

CONTENTS

GRETA GERWIG'S 2019 adaptation of *Little Women* stars, from left, Emma Watson as Meg March, Florence Pugh as Amy March, Saoirse Ronan as Jo March, and Eliza Scanlen as Beth March.

INTRODUCTION

Changing the Landscape Forever

TAPPING INTO THE INNER LIVES OF GIRLS, AND TREATING THOSE LIVES SERIOUSLY, LOUISA MAY ALCOTT TOLD A BOLD, BEAUTIFUL STORY THAT WAS BUILT TO LAST AND LAST

BY GINA MCINTYRE

ASK A DEVOTED FAN OF LOUISA May Alcott's *Little Women* to identify a favorite moment in the book, and you might get any number of responses.

There's the time Jo accidentally singes the hair off her older sister, Meg, as she's helping Meg prepare for a social engagement. Or the time young, artistic Amy accidentally plasters herself into a bucket as she's attempting to make a cast of her foot. There are the amateur dramatic productions the sisters stage inside their humble home—swashbuckling tales of high adventure. And there are the comically combative encounters with their wealthy, outspoken Aunt March, who has no compunction about expressing her disapproval over their somewhat unconventional lifestyle.

Then there are the heartbreaking tragedies and daily hardships that befall the girls: death, for one thing, as well as the daunting challenges of marriage and motherhood, fraught relationships, and unrequited romantic love.

Drawing inspiration from her own life with three sisters, Alcott—who was born in 1832 and lived in an environment of financial tenuousness, burgeoning philosophical ideas, and then the Civil War—presented an honest, insightful collection of anecdotes that chronicled the passage from adolescence into adulthood for these four girls (and their mother, Marmee), each of whom presented her own distinctive model of womanhood. With that, Alcott created a runaway best-seller—the book was written in two parts; the first installment was so successful when it was published in 1868 that Alcott quickly produced a follow-up that was released the next year.

Alcott also forever changed the landscape of literary fiction. Taking the inner lives of girls seriously at that time amounted to a revolutionary act, and her nuanced, sensitive depiction of each of the sisters is part of what has led to the book's remarkable staying power. At the story's heart is the rebellious Jo, an aspiring writer who resents the notion that she should

LOUISA M. ALCOTT

AUTHOR OF

"LITTLE WOMEN"

EMMA WATSON AS MEG WITH filmmaker Greta Gerwig on the set of 2019's *Little Women*.

marry and instead longs to pursue her creative passions; she remains indelible among literary heroines.

Jo's hunger for life, her principled recalcitrance, and her determination to live on her own terms have resonated across the ages in ways the author could never have anticipated. Alcott has become the godmother of some of modern culture's most significant voices: Simone de Beauvoir, Gloria Steinem, J.K. Rowling, and numerous others. It's rare to find a novel that has spoken so strongly to so many disparate thinkers.

The novel has touched every corner of American culture, inspiring books, movies, plays, operas, and various other sorts of interpretations and adaptations—including Oscar-nominated director and screenwriter Greta Gerwig's new movie, with Saoirse Ronan in the role of Jo.

The story is beloved by readers around the world who have embraced Alcott's deeply moral, emotionally complex tale, and many of whom have traveled to visit Orchard House, the Massachusetts home where she wrote *Little Women*. Today the house is a museum, a powerful time capsule of 19th-century life, and the fact that it continues to thrive is another testament to Alcott's long-lasting appeal.

"It's really about mothers, grandmothers, aunts, teachers, librarians passing this book down to the younger generation," says Anne Boyd Rioux, a professor of English at the University of New Orleans and the author of 2018's *Meg, Jo, Beth, Amy: The Story of Little Women and Why It Still Matters.* "It's never been called the great American novel or anything like that, although it should be considered for that. Instead it's been part of the underground, shadow canon, if you will, for female writers. It's a book that's been considered a rite of passage, I think, in growing up for girls. This is a book that will show you what your options are and to help you find yourself."

If not for her own lineage, family life, and surroundings, Alcott might

"LOUISE ALCOTT"
THE CHILDREN'S FRIEND.
LITTLE WOMEN
Lizbeth B. Comins

AN 1888 ILLUSTRATION depicts Alcott reading *Little Women* to children.

never have delivered such a compelling portrayal of life in the March household. Jo's sisters and mother were fictionalized versions of Alcott's own family. The fictional Mr. March and the real-life Amos Bronson Alcott, Louisa's father, both had progressive attitudes toward women's education and equality.

"Louisa was, by nature, a fighter whose rebellious spirit pervades *Little Women,*" says Eve LaPlante, the author of *Marmee & Louisa: The Untold Story of Louisa May Alcott and Her Mother* as well as a cousin of Louisa May Alcott's and a great niece of Louisa's mother, Abigail. "Louisa hated the limitations placed on her as a girl. She wanted to run; girls weren't allowed. She wanted an education; only her male friends and cousins got that. She wanted to enlist to fight in the Civil War; women weren't allowed. She wanted to vote . . . The list goes on. I think all that pain was funneled into *Little Women,* a cry of the heart fueled by Louisa's desire to change things, to reform the world."

Raised with the foundational belief that women were equal to men and just as entitled to speak their minds and follow their hearts, Louisa evangelized her feminist philosophy to anyone she encountered, and imbued that message into her most enduring narrative. *Little Women* encourages us all to live up to our potential, to pursue our dreams, and to embrace life to the fullest, no matter the obstacles we encounter—and reminds us to always, always hold close the ones we love.

Writing circa 1878 to a reader who had written to her seeking guidance, Alcott responded: "I can only say to you as I do to the many young writers who ask for advice—there is no easy road to successful authorship; it has to be earned by long and patient labor, many disappointments, uncertainties and trials. We all have our own life to pursue, Our own kind of dream to be weaving... And we all have the power To make wishes come true, As long as we keep believing." ●

CHAPTER I

The Creator: Louisa May Alcott

Living in New England through the heart of the 19th century—and the Civil War—the author of *Little Women* and its sequels created a milieu suited to its time, while also delivering a forward-thinking heroine (based on herself) who remains an inspiration today

A LITERARY REVOLUTIONARY

WITH HER FAMILY'S SUPPORT, AND HER OWN DETERMINATION, LOUISA MAY ALCOTT UNSPOOLED A CHARACTER-RICH NARRATIVE THAT MADE HER A SENSATION FOR THE REST OF HER LIFE

FEW NOVELS HAVE enjoyed the longevity or influence of Louisa May Alcott's *Little Women*. Published more than 150 years ago, the story of four sisters and their journey from adolescence into adulthood in 19th-century Massachusetts has become a towering classic. Alongside Jane Austen's *Pride and Prejudice, Little Women* has been embraced by generations of women as a rite of passage, both for its exploration of family dynamics and its insights into the tender bonds shared among siblings.

It's beloved, too, for its heroine, Jo March, a character determined to defy societal convention and pursue her own path. Although she finds love, she's much more defined by her commitment to her writing at a time when it was socially unacceptable for women to devote themselves to careers over marriage. Famously, Jo, the character who inspired dozens of other women to pursue creative careers, is the stand-in for Alcott herself—a writer above all things who cast aside societal norms and instead held true to what she felt in her heart was right.

"She rejected the conventional 19th-century role of wife and mother and instead embraced the possibility of liberty and control over her own economic fate," said Susan Cheever, the author of 2011's *Louisa May Alcott: A Personal Biography,* in a 2014 interview with Library of America. "As a result, Alcott collided with society's rules about the place of women in the world."

That audacious, progressive viewpoint was, in many ways, her birthright.

EARLY DAYS

Born on November 29, 1832, in Germantown, Pennsylvania, Louisa was the second child of Amos Bronson Alcott and his wife Abigail "Abba" May Alcott, who shared a commitment to social justice. Bronson, as he

LOUISA MAY ALCOTT, circa 1870. Opposite: A childhood portrait.

AMOS BRONSON ALCOTT IN Concord, Massachusetts, left. From this bench at the base of an elm tree in front of Orchard House, he would greet and converse with passersby on Lexington Road. Here: The Alcotts at Orchard House in 1865; Louisa is seated on the ground, while her mother, Abigail May Alcott, stands with her eldest daughter, Anna Alcott Pratt, Anna's son Frederick in the stroller, and Bronson Alcott. This is only existing image of most of the family together.

was known, was a radical thinker and philosopher, a contemporary of literary luminaries Henry David Thoreau and Ralph Waldo Emerson. Like them, he was a member of the transcendentalist movement, which taught that divinity could be found in nature. Abba was herself a gifted intellectual and vocal supporter of women's rights. She later became one of Massachusetts's first professional social workers.

When Louisa was two, the family moved to Boston, the first relocation of many for the Alcott clan. A gifted orator, Bronson put his skills to use as an educator. He founded the Temple School in 1834 on Tremont Street in Boston, where he encouraged students to interact with the physical world and to ask questions about coursework rather than stick to a script of rote memorization. Corporal punishment, common in many schools then, was forbidden.

To supplement the school's staff, Bronson hired transcendentalist colleagues Elizabeth Peabody and Margaret Fuller—the former was a pioneering educator who went on to open the first English-language kindergarten in the United States; the latter was a prominent journalist and an early advocate of feminist ideals. But not everyone in the community responded favorably to their approach. After the school admitted a young African American girl, other parents withdrew their children, forcing the institution to close after six years.

Louisa, meanwhile, was being

A 19TH-CENTURY DRAWING depicting Louisa and her family in their Concord home. Bottom left, the Alcott sisters brought this "autograph fan" to dances and would have friends sign it; the signature "L. M. Alcott" is the fifth from the right. Bottom right, a rendering of Bronson Alcott's Concord School of Philosophy as it appeared in the 1880s.

educated in the family home in Concord. She once wrote, "I never went to school except to my father or such governesses as from time to time came into the family . . . so we had lessons each morning in the study. And very happy hours they were to us, for my father taught in the wise way which unfolds what lies in the child's nature as a flower blooms, rather than crammed in, like a Strasburg goose, with more than it could digest."

FROM FRUITLANDS TO ORCHARD HOUSE

Determined to continue to live by his principles, Bronson, with Englishman Charles Lane, founded a utopian society in the hopes of building a peaceful community that would mark a return to the Garden of Eden. Dubbed Fruitlands, the commune opened in June of 1843, on 100 acres in Harvard, Massachusetts, and was home to just 14 people, including 10-year-old Louisa and her three sisters, Anna, Elizabeth, and Abigail. But it was a difficult life. They wore no wool or cotton (as those were products of capitalism) and doused themselves in icy water to develop resistance against "severe weather."

"One of the most important aspects of their communal life involved diet—in fact, what we would call a vegan diet, with no animal products, dairy products, or anything like that," Richard Francis, author of *Fruitlands: The Alcott Family and Their Search for Utopia,* said in an interview with Boston public radio station WBUR. "They tended to eat a lot of apples . . . and whatever vegetables and fruit they could get hold of in season."

With Bronson often traveling to give lectures, much of the work around the homestead fell to Louisa's mother, Abba. When the weather turned unexpectedly harsh, the project proved too difficult to maintain, and after just six months, it was abandoned altogether, leaving the family to search once more for a new place to call home. "As Louisa put it, [Bronson] was a man in a balloon, with his family holding the ropes trying to hold him down to earth," Harriet Reisen, author of *Louisa May Alcott: The Woman Behind Little Women,* told NPR in 2009. "He seemed to live on air, and in the air, and had no concern about earning a living. It didn't seem to bother him that his family was literally starving."

Meanwhile, teenage Louisa already had discovered her passion for writing, and she soon realized her avocation could help turn around her family's financial fortunes. By the time the Alcotts had settled in Boston in 1849, she had begun to write thrillers that she hoped to sell, but to provide for the family she also worked as a governess and mended laundry. Finally, in 1851, she published her first poem, "Sunlight" in *Peterson's Magazine* under the pen name Flora Fairfield; three years later followed a collection of original fairy tales and poems, *Flower Fables.*

In 1856, however, tragedy struck—Louisa's younger sister Elizabeth "Lizzie" Sewall Alcott contracted scarlet fever. Although she survived, her illness prompted the family to once again relocate to Concord. Bronson purchased a ramshackle property that included two early 19th-century houses on a 12-acre apple orchard located just two miles from Walden Pond. They dubbed the residence Orchard House. Lizzie, though, never had the chance to live there. She suffered a relapse and died in March of 1858 at age 22.

A month after her passing, Louisa wrote in her journal: "I don't miss her as I expected to do, for she seems nearer and dearer than before; and I am glad to know she is safe from pain and age in some world where her innocent soul must be happy."

Louisa moved into Orchard House to help comfort her grieving mother while Bronson made modifications to the family home. One of his additions would become especially momentous. In Louisa's upstairs bedroom, Bronson built a tiny wooden writing surface, no bigger than a lap desk, adjacent to the window sill. It was at this desk that

Scene in the Balcony of the Hotel.

AN ILLUSTRATION DEPICTING Louisa as she finds a poster advertising her pseudonymously written story "Bertha," published in the *Saturday Evening Gazette* in 1856, above. Left: "Scene in the Balcony of the Hotel," from "Pauline's Passion and Punishment," which was published in two parts in *Frank Leslie's Illustrated Newspaper* in January 1863. Opposite, Louisa at her desk in Orchard House.

Louisa May Alcott would write many of the pages of *Little Women.*

THE ROAD TO LITERARY CELEBRITY

The Alcott family seemed in position to enjoy some stability. But when the Civil War broke out, Louisa felt called to lend her aid to the Union cause. She served as a nurse at a Georgetown hospital, but her tenure came to a premature and abrupt end after she contracted typhoid fever. She returned home in 1862 to recuperate with her family, but the harrowing experiences she witnessed left an indelible mark and became the foundation for her first published book, 1863's *Hospital Sketches.*

"That was a huge milestone in her work—she always said that book 'showed me my style,'" says Daniel Shealy, a professor of English at University of North Carolina Charlotte, who has edited or coedited 12 books about Louisa May Alcott. "She's able to take firsthand experiences and turn them into a story, into a narrative. In doing so, she is able to take horrific scenes, and infuse these scenes with truth, realism, but also humor. I think that she saw that as very important in her writing, the ability to do both of those. In many ways that helped shape her career as she moved forward."

Hospital Sketches was an unqualified success, yet Louisa continued to write lurid thrillers under the pen name A.M Barnard. They were simply more lucrative than her other projects. *Pauline's Passion and Punishment,* for example, was published in 1863 in *Frank Leslie's Illustrated Newsletter* and earned Louisa $100, about $2,000 today. "They were the bodice-rippers of the era," says Anne Boyd Rioux, professor of English at the University of New Orleans and the author of 2018's *Meg, Jo, Beth, Amy: The Story of Little Women and Why It Still Matters.* "They were really racy for the 19th century. We're talking drug use. We're talking incest, all kinds of people lusting after each other. She had a lot of fun writing them, and it made her a lot of money, much more than she got for publishing a story or a poem in the *Atlantic Monthly* for instance."

Louisa's growing renown, and income, only underscored her conviction that she had no need for, and no interest in, finding a husband. She was far happier remaining unmarried and able to direct the course of her own life without compromise. "I'd rather be a free spinster and paddle my own canoe," Alcott famously said. In 1864, her book *Moods* saw her continue to mature as a writer, with a story centered on an adventure-seeking tomboy who marries the wrong man. Her most iconic work followed soon after.

Little Women was actually a commission: Thomas Niles of Roberts Brothers Publishers asked Louisa to write a story for girls, and despite some reluctance, she agreed. Inspired by her own childhood and adolescence, she invented the four loving sisters of the fictional March family—responsible Meg; aspiring author Jo; fragile, ailing Beth; and ambitious social climber Amy, who live together in Concord with their adored mother, Marmee, poor but happy.

"The only reason she [writes *Little Women*] is for money," Rioux says. "The whole book is informed by this struggle, this need. There's some great passages where Jo talks about money giving her power and independence and really feeling that sense of pride when she's able to provide for Beth's care. Writing and needing to make money are all wrapped up together in Alcott's life and are embedded throughout *Little Women.*"

After the first volume of *Little Women* appeared in 1868, money was never again an issue for Alcott. The book was a sensation, selling out every copy and prompting Roberts Brothers to ask for the second volume. The follow-up, which centered on the sisters' lives as they enter adulthood, arrived one year later and sold just as well. A second follow-up, *Little Men,* was

MISS ALCOTT BEFORE THE REGISTRAR.

An eye witness reports the appearance of Louisa M. Alcott before the Selectmen of Concord to secure registration for herself. It was several weeks ago. Miss Alcott meant to register early. She said to the authority, "I want to have my name put on the register that I may vote for School Committee." "Very well," said the Selectman. "Have you brought your receipt for your last year's tax?" "No," said Miss Alcott, "I did not know it was necessary." "You will have to bring it." "Won't this year's tax receipt do just as well?" "Oh, yes, but you have not paid it."

Miss Alcott runs over with mirth. A little comical look came on her face, as she said, "I never did hanker to pay my taxes, but now I am in a hurry to pay them." The Selectman, as much amused as Miss Alcott, got the tax bill made out by the Assessor, and then and there Miss Alcott paid it. When they put her name on the Register, it was found that Miss Alcott had been the first woman to register in the old town of Concord. Since that time several meetings have been held, and other names added. But it seemed right that that of Miss Alcott should lead all the rest. W.

LOUISA M. ALCOTT'S FAMOUS BOOKS

HOSPITAL SKETCHES. Price, $1.50.

ROBERTS BROTHERS, *Publishers, Boston.*

published in 1871 to strong sales.

Louisa had officially become a literary phenomenon.

"I think there was the feeling that what you were holding in your hands wasn't just a good book, but was a story that was alive," Rioux says. "These girls . . . leap off the page, first because they're based on real people, and secondly because that's Louisa May Alcott's genius. The dialogue she writes—they talked about it being so fresh and being so real and true. This kind of writing wasn't that common. We talk always about Mark Twain inventing American literature with the language that he used in *Huckleberry Finn.* Louisa May Alcott was doing something very similar, but 16 years earlier."

WOMEN'S SUFFRAGE

Perhaps unsurprisingly, Alcott used her success to both care for her family and to advocate for causes in which she strongly believed. "Louisa combined the best aspects of both her parents," said John Matteson, the Pulitzer Prize–winning author of 2008's *Eden's Outcasts: The Story of Louisa May Alcott and Her Father,* in an interview with the *Hartford Courant.* "She was a moral idealist, like her father, but she was also a fighter like her mother. When she found a cause she believed in, she became a fury on its behalf."

Women's suffrage was a huge focus for Alcott. When the state of Massachusetts passed a law in 1879 allowing women the right to vote in local elections on issues involving children and education, Louisa organized reading groups to educate potential voters and distributed petitions encouraging them to go to the polls. When she was met with resistance—some women said they were too busy running their households to worry about politics—she took to her journal to express her frustration, writing, "Trying to stir up the women about Suffrage. So timid & slow . . . Drove about & drummed up women to my Suffrage meeting. So hard to move people out of the old ruts."

On March 29, 1880, Alcott attended the Concord Town Meeting and, along with 19 other women, officially cast her ballot. After the women voted, Alcott reported, "No bolt fell on our audacious heads, no earthquake shook the town." Still, history had been made. "I like to help women help themselves, as that is, in my opinion, the best way to settle the woman question," Alcott said. "Whatever we can do and do well we have a right to, and

FROM LEFT: AN ARTICLE IN *The Woman's Journal*, August 23, 1879, about Louisa's voter registration efforts; an illustration of Civil War nurse Tribulation Periwinkle, Alcott's alter ego from *Hospital Sketches*; and Union Hotel Hospital, in Washington, D.C., where Louisa served as a nurse in December 1862.

I don't think any one will deny us."

Louisa continued to work—both on the causes that were important to her and on her writing—up until her death. The final book featuring heroine Jo March, *Jo's Boys,* was published in 1886, two years before a stroke claimed Louisa's life at age 55 in March of 1888. Even in the end, her fortunes were forever entwined with her family's—her death came only two days after that of her father, Bronson, and she was buried with her sisters in Sleepy Hollow Cemetery in Concord. "The loss of this talented writer will be felt far and wide among the many readers of her favorite books," the *New York Times* wrote in her obituary, published March 7, 1888.

Her legacy is as remarkable as any she might have dreamed up for her heroines. Louisa is remembered as an unconventional, flawed, passionate woman fully invested with spirit, zeal for life, and an abiding decency of character that's especially inspirational today.

"As with Harriet Beecher Stowe, you can't read Alcott without feeling inspired to be better than you are," Matteson told the *Hartford Courant.* "It's funny . . . many of the authors we consider great have a deep sense of moral ambiguity: Melville, Dostoyevsky, Goethe. Alcott never had much doubt as to right and wrong. Perhaps that makes her somewhat less of an artist, but reading her can be a wonderfully strengthening experience." ●

TRANSCENDENT THOUGHTS

That her father was a colleague of Emerson and Thoreau, and shared their transcendental philosophy, helped shape Alcott's views

LIKE THE OTHER members of her family, Louisa May Alcott was a radical, progressive thinker—an abolitionist, an environmentalist, and a strong proponent of equal rights for women. Many of her most closely held beliefs were rooted in the ideals of the transcendentalist philosophy, which originated in New England in the early 1800s and held that divinity can be seen in all of nature and humanity.

"That philosophy was crucial to her development as an individual, in the sense that it advocated self-reliance, it advocated an individual's unique gifts—each individual was a divine being," says Daniel Shealy, a professor of English at the University of North Carolina Charlotte and a longtime Alcott scholar. "That certainly had to influence her growing up, as did the whole culture of self-reform. How do you become the best person that you can be? How do you live in a world with others and help others?"

Ralph Waldo Emerson and Henry David Thoreau are the writers most typically associated with the movement—*Walden,* Thoreau's account of the two years he spent living in a cabin on the northern shore of Walden Pond, is the definitive transcendentalist text—but Louisa's father, Bronson Alcott, was also one of its founding fathers. He routinely entertained Emerson and Thoreau in his study at Orchard House, and he raised Louisa according to transcendentalist ideals.

"Her father really believed that every child was born with a divine genius," says Anne Boyd Rioux, a professor of English at the University of New Orleans and the author of *Meg, Jo, Beth, Amy: The Story of Little Women and Why It Still Matters.* "Each of the girls had their own talent, the thing they were interested in, and their parents always encouraged them in it. I think without transcendentalism, if her parents were conforming to the mores of the day, we wouldn't have *Little Women.*"

As with most things, Louisa preferred to follow her own path, so while she espoused the movement's chief tenets, she also viewed the idealistic philosophy with a healthy amount of skepticism—no doubt owing to the uncomfortable months she'd spent living on her father's failed commune, Fruitlands. (In 1873, she published a satirical account of her time at Fruitlands titled *Transcendental Wild Oats,* about an idealistic dreamer who leads his family into folly by attempting to live according to exacting principles while those around him suffer.)

"I think she could see the humor in it to some degree," Shealy says. "She could see [what happens when] the idealism [is] carried to the extreme, ignoring the realities of life. I think she saw that with her own family. It's great to have high ideal thoughts, but there needs to be food on the table." ●

WALDEN.

BY HENRY D. THOREAU,

AUTHOR OF "A WEEK ON THE CONCORD AND MERRIMACK RIVERS."

I [illegible] pose to write an ode to dejection, but to brag as lustily as chanticleer in the [illegible]ning, standing on his roost, if only to wake my neighbors up. — Page [illegible]

WALDEN POND, AND THE title page from Henry David Thoreau's *Walden*, written on those shores, opposite. Here, a circa 1920 illustration showing a young Louisa May Alcott in the library with Ralph Waldo Emerson, who was a close friend of her father's and a formative influence on her work.

They all drew to the fire, mother in the big chair, with Beth at her feet; Meg and Amy perched on either arm of the chair, and Jo leaning on the back. — PAGE 12.

LITTLE WOMEN

OR,

MEG, JO, BETH AND AMY

BY LOUISA M. ALCOTT

ILLUSTRATED BY MAY ALCOTT

BOSTON
ROBERTS BROTHERS
1868

THE STORY OF LITTLE WOMEN

HOW THE NOVEL CAME INTO BEING, WHAT IT CONTAINED, AND WHY IT UPENDED THE WORLD OF BOOKS, LITERATURE, AND SOCIETY

WHEN THOMAS Niles Jr., a partner at Roberts Brothers Publishers, asked Louisa May Alcott to write "a story for girls," the author didn't exactly spark to the idea. At that point in her career, Alcott had enjoyed modest success writing under her own name—and spinning risqué, tawdry yarns under the pseudonym A.M. Barnard.

Alcott's reservations about writing for a juvenile audience, specifically girls, owed to the fact that, as she herself said, she had "never liked girls or [known] many" other than her three siblings: her older sister, Anna, and

THE FRONTISPIECE AND TITLE page of the first edition of *Little Women*, opposite. Louisa's youngest sister, May, provided four illustrations for the edition. Here: An undated illustration by M.V. Wheelhouse of the March sisters at home.

her younger sisters, Lizzie and May. She though it unlikely that a novel based on the "queer plays and experiences" that the four of them had shared would be of interest. Nevertheless, when the first volume of *Little Women* arrived months later, on September 30, 1868, a literary phenomenon was born.

"It probably had as big an effect on children's literature as Harry Potter really did today," says Daniel Shealy, the professor of English at the University of North Carolina Charlotte who edited Alcott's journals and letters. "It really is the first book, at least in American literature, to treat teenagers as real people. It really was a leap forward in realism for children's literature. The literature that came after that, you see the influences of *Little Women.*"

Told as a collection of moving vignettes rather than a more conventional narrative, the book opens with the four daughters of the March family knitting together in the family home in front of the fire on Christmas Eve in their Concord, Massachusetts, home. Within the first four sentences, Louisa has introduced the sisters with brief declarations that also serve as succinct portraits of each girl.

"Christmas won't be Christmas without any presents," grumbled Jo, lying on the rug.

"It's so dreadful to be poor!" sighed Meg, looking down at her old dress.

"I don't think it's fair for some girls to have plenty of pretty things, and other girls nothing at all," added little Amy, with an injured sniff.

"We've got Father and Mother, and each other," said Beth contentedly from her corner.

Alcott goes on to detail each of the siblings, describing 16-year-old Meg, whose given name is Margaret, as "very pretty, being plump and fair, with large eyes, plenty of soft brown hair, a sweet mouth, and white hands, of which she was rather vain." Next is 15-year-old Josephine, who prefers to go by the boyish "Jo" and is "very tall, thin, and brown" with "a decided mouth, a comical nose, and sharp, gray eyes, which

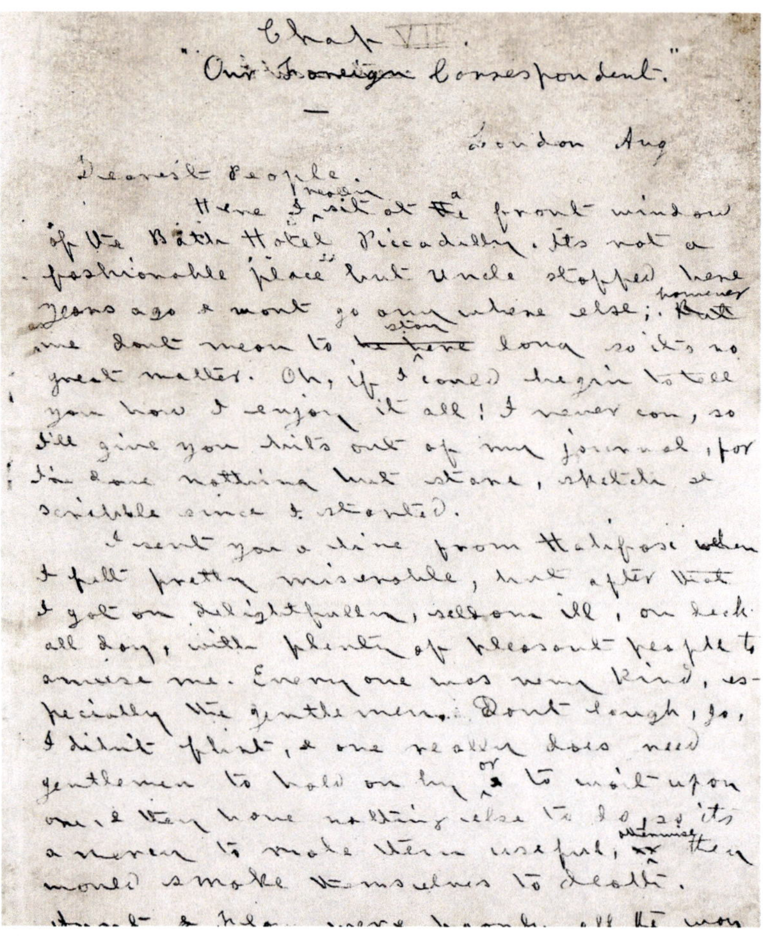

Chap VIII.
"Our Foreign Correspondent."

London Aug

Dearest People.
Here I mean sit at the front window of the Bath Hotel Piccadilly. Its not a fashionable place but uncle stopped here years ago & wont go anywhere else; however we dont mean to stay long so it's no great matter. Oh, if I could begin to tell you how I enjoy it all! I never can, so I'll give you bits out of my journal, for I've done nothing but stare, sketch & scribble since I started.

I sent you a line from Halifax when I felt pretty miserable, but after that I got on delightfully, seldom ill, on deck all day, with plenty of pleasant people to amuse me. Every one was very kind, especially the gentlemen. Dont laugh, Jo, I didn't flirt, & one really does need gentlemen to hold on by or to wait upon one, & they have nothing else to do so its a mercy to make them useful, otherwise they would smoke themselves to death.

Little Women. **By Louisa M. Alcott. 2 volumes in one, with illustrations.** Given for one new name, and 25 cts. additional.

Until now we have been unable to offer this charming story for less than four names. Now we offer it for one name, and 25 cts. additional.

Little Women! Who has not read about them? Who does not want to read about them again? Let us recall their names, — Meg, Jo, Beth and Amy. The story and its author need no further introduction.

We now give these two volumes in one for one new name, and 25 cts. additional, instead of for four new names. Price now only $1.10. Former price, $3. **Postage and packing, 15 cts.,** when sent as a premium or purchased.

A MANUSCRIPT PAGE FROM ***Little Women*****, opposite, top, and, bottom, an 1890 advertisement from "Popular Books for Girls and the Family." Here: A circa 1940 lithograph depicting the girls performing their Christmas play.**

appeared to see everything, and were by turns fierce, funny, or thoughtful." Elizabeth, or Beth, is a "rosy, smooth-haired, bright-eyed girl of thirteen, with a shy manner, a timid voice, and a peaceful expression"; Amy, the youngest is "a regular snow maiden, with blue eyes, and yellow hair curling on her shoulders, pale and slender, and always carrying herself like a young lady mindful of her manners."

Although once a family of some social standing, the Marches now live a life of reduced circumstances, but they are not, over the whole, unhappy. They spend their days together with their beloved mother, whom they adoringly refer to as Marmee, dutifully tending to their responsibilities but also making time for artistic pursuits—for Meg, it's acting; for Beth, it's music; for Amy, it's art; and for fierce, headstrong Jo, it is writing. She spends hours in the confines of her attic putting her thoughts to paper, determined never to wed lest her husband expect her to put down her pen someday.

Jo's life is complicated by her relationship with Theodore Laurence, the wealthy young orphan who lives with his distant grandfather in the opulent home adjacent to the March property. Jo refers to him affectionately as "Teddy," and they become inseparable. He, too, is a rebellious spirit, and he falls madly in love with Jo, though he initially keeps his feelings for her secret. Laurie, as he's more commonly known, becomes like extended family; his grandfather takes a shine to sweet Beth and invites her to come play their grand piano whenever she likes. Laurie's tutor, Mr. Brooke, becomes terribly fond of Meg, even if he is similarly shy to declare his affections.

The early chapters center largely on the daily exploits of the girls, but there are life-altering events, too. Beth develops scarlet fever, which nearly kills her. The family receives a troubling telegram that Mr. March, who has been away ministering to Civil War soldiers, is gravely ill, forcing Marmee to travel to Washington, D.C., to be by his side. To pay for her trip, Jo sacrifices her "one beauty," cutting her hair and selling it for money. Amy burns a draft of Jo's novel in a fit of jealousy; attempting to make amends, she follows Jo and Laurie to the pond where they are skating, only to fall through the ice into the frigid waters below. When her sister is rescued and safely back at home, Jo is deeply ashamed that she was reluctant to forgive Amy for destroying her book.

In both good times and bad, *Little Women*'s authentic depiction of the lives of young girls, their concerns, their aspirations, their imperfections was nothing short of groundbreaking.

THIS PERCY TARRANT ILLUSTRATION, opposite, depicts Amy's rescue by Laurie after falling through the ice. Above: A May Alcott illustration from the first edition of *Little Women*, "Meg Goes to Vanity Fair."

MACASSAR OIL

"It was virtually unheard of to have a girl in a book who wasn't a caricature or a stereotype or meant to symbolize or represent some vice or virtue of her sex," says Anne Boyd Rioux, professor of English at the University of New Orleans and the author of 2018's *Meg, Jo, Beth, Amy: The Story of Little Women and Why It Still Matters.* "A girl could never just be a person. What we see in these girls instead is that they have flaws, but that doesn't doom them. They're complicated, and their relationships are messy. It was one of the first American books that felt real on the page."

Jo in particular was a singular literary heroine—loving and loyal but also bold, angry, defiant, and resentful of the idea that women were universally expected to surrender their independence and live instead for their husbands and children. "The portrayals of women artists were really negative at the time," Rioux says. "Jo, on the other hand, was given so much encouragement by her family. She never once feels ashamed or guilty about the time she's spending on her own writing her stories. That is virtually unheard of in 19th-century literature. Girls were made to feel bad for doing anything for themselves. Wanting to shine and wanting to have a talent that was recognized, that was considered vain and selfish. It was very unladylike."

Readers couldn't get enough. The first print run of *Little Women* numbered some 2,000 copies. It sold out in days, becoming a runaway literary

BRITISH ARTIST HAROLD Copping imagined the scene in which Jo sells her hair to pay for her mother to bring Mr. March home, opposite. Above: An illustration by M.V. Wheelhouse shows Jo tending to Beth, left, and another by Copping shows Beth missing her mother while she is away; the book's caption reads, "She hid her face in the folds of a certain dear old gown, and made her little moan."

sensation beyond anything Alcott might have imagined. A reviewer in *Eclectic Magazine* called it "the very best of books to reach the hearts of the young of any age from six to sixty."

Alcott was then asked to augment her original 23 chapters, which she used as an opportunity to take the narrative in a somewhat more mature direction. "Alcott's really after something different in book two," says Shealy. "I really think she set out to write a modern marriage novel in book two, and to deal with a lot more serious issues."

In the second volume, published in 1869, Meg marries Laurie's former tutor John Brooke, and they have two young children, twins, a boy called Demi, short for Demijohn, and a girl called Daisy. But the couple struggles financially and with the toll that caring for children can take on a relationship. Amy travels to Europe with family benefactor Aunt March to further her study of art and briefly considers marrying wealthy English suitor Fred Vaughn, in pursuit of a comfortable life, while back at home, Beth's poor health continues to decline. Eventually, she slips away, leaving Jo inconsolable.

Alcott's most controversial narrative choice, however, involved the fate of Laurie and Jo. Readers had longed for the two friends to live together in bliss, but Alcott was dead set against that idea. "I won't marry Jo to Laurie to please anyone," she wrote in her journal. In a letter to a friend, the author elaborated on her plans for the character who was so clearly her literary avatar. "Jo should have remained a literary spinster but so many enthusiastic young ladies wrote to me clamorously demanding that she should marry Laurie, or somebody, that I didn't dare refuse & out of perversity went & made a funny match for her."

So, in *Little Women*'s second volume, Jo rejects Laurie's proposal, insisting that they are far too much alike to make a solid match and leaving him utterly heartbroken. He departs for Europe; meanwhile, Jo, working as a governess in New York, meets a kindly German professor, Friedrich Bhaer, whose serious demeanor and admirable intellect win her heart.

"[Alcott's] toeing the line," Rioux says. "She's saying, 'Okay. Fine. If I'm crossing the line to marry her, I'm going to do something very different than what you're expecting and give her instead an intellectual companion.' She describes him as a warm fire. Professor Bhaer, he represents something very different than Laurie would represent. This isn't romance with a capital *R,* sweep me off my feet, and ride off into the sunset. Their whole love scene is full of dropping things and making mistakes and feeling awkward. It's really refreshing, I think."

BETH GREETING MR. MARCH as he returns from war, above, an illustration by May Alcott from the first edition. Opposite: Preparing for Meg's wedding.

AN ILLUSTRATION FROM **Alcott's *Good Wives*, left. Below, the frontispiece and title page of *Little Men*. Opposite: An undated illustration sees Professor Bhaer observing Jo with children.**

"These were the boys, and they lived together as happily as twelve lads could; studying and playing, working and squabbling, fighting faults and cultivating virtues, in the good old-fashioned way." —Page 28.

LITTLE MEN:

LIFE AT PLUMFIELD WITH JO'S BOYS.

BY

LOUISA M. ALCOTT,

AUTHOR OF "LITTLE WOMEN," "AN OLD-FASHIONED GIRL," "HOSPITAL SKETCHES."

BOSTON:
ROBERTS BROTHERS.
1871.

In the end, Laurie does find happiness with a March girl—he marries Jo's sister Amy. The youngest March girl had been secretly carrying a torch for Laurie for nearly her entire life and is happy to act as a society bride who can tame his wilder instincts.

"It is fascinating because Amy is happy to conform because there are things that she wants and she knows she can get by doing that," Rioux says. "Jo can't do it to save her life."

The novel concludes with Jo Bhaer having inherited the Plumfield estate from the family's wealthy benefactor Aunt March. She and Friedrich establish a school for boys, and together they have two sons of their own, stalling Jo's plans for literary stardom. *Little Women*'s final pages flash forward to Jo and her sisters cheerfully discussing the ways in which their lives turned out very differently than they expected: "I haven't given up the hope that I may write a good book yet, but I can wait, and I'm sure it will be all the better for such experiences," Jo declares.

Readers eagerly devoured the second volume of Alcott's saga, turning it into even more of a blockbuster than its predecessor—quite simply, everyone was reading *Little Women*.

"Girls may have been the primary readers, but by all accounts it was also read by boys, by young men, others," Shealy says.

"[There's] a wonderful anecdote by a friend of Alcott's, who is talking about the publication of part two... He talked about how everyone at his office was reading it, down to the elevator boy. It really was the hit of the season."

Little Women gave Alcott a wealth that put her in a unique position to provide for her beloved family, and she continued writing about the adventures of the March clan until the end of her days. *Little Men, or Life at Plumfield with Jo's Boys* was published in 1871; *Jo's Boys, and How They Turned Out: A Sequel to Little Men* came out in 1886, two years before her death.

For Shealy, the stories of the March family, and really all of Alcott's fiction, remains vital for its well-drawn characters and the way they rise to the challenges of life with dignity and compassion.

"Alcott's work teaches compassion," he says. "It teaches self-sacrifice. It teaches adjustment to the world around us. Even though our dreams might not come true... what then can you do? How do you go on? Readers today, young people today, take away these ideas from this book." ●

REALITY BASED

JO MARCH WAS PRACTICALLY AN ALTER EGO FOR LOUISA MAY ALCOTT. OTHER *LITTLE WOMEN* CHARACTERS BORE CLOSE RESEMBLANCES TO OTHER ALCOTTS.

MR. MARCH
➛ BRONSON ALCOTT

Born November 29, 1799 (33 years before Louisa's birthday on the same date), in Wolcott, Connecticut, Amos Bronson Alcott gained celebrity in his day as a progressive philosopher and teacher who embraced transcendentalism and often entertained the icons of the movement in his study. His intellectual pursuits, as noble as they might have been, created hardships for his family—he traveled extensively, often leaving his wife and daughters to scrape by financially. His legacy as an educator, however, is important. He encouraged students to ask questions of their instructors and to engage in hands-on learning by interacting with the natural world; he also was strongly opposed to corporal punishment. He died in Boston on March 4, 1888.

MARMEE
➛ ABIGAIL "ABBA" MAY ALCOTT

In *Little Women,* the March sisters idolize their mother as an unending source of encouragement, love, and support, and Abba inspired the same devotion among her four daughters. (She gave Louisa her first fountain pen on her 14th birthday, encouraging her to write "to obtain self-possession and purpose.") Abba was a vocal proponent of equal rights for women, the abolition of slavery, and temperance, and she devoted herself to bettering the circumstances of others, becoming one of the first paid social workers in the state of Massachusetts in 1848. She died November 25, 1877, prompting Louisa to write in her journal, "I never wish her back, but a great warmth seems gone out of life . . . She was so loyal, tender, and true, life was hard for her and no one knew all she had to bear but her children."

MEG

➛ ANNA ALCOTT PRATT

The eldest of the Alcott sisters, Anna was born March 16, 1831, and like her fictional counterpart, initially harbored dreams of a life on the stage; together she and Louisa were founding members of the Concord Dramatic Union in 1858. Also like Meg, Anna worked as a governess before falling in love—in Anna's case with John Bridge Pratt, also a member of the acting troupe. They married in 1860. Louisa was disappointed with the news of their engagement, writing in her journal: "I moaned in private over my great loss, and said I'd never forgive J. for taking Anna from me; but I shall if he makes her happy, and turn to little May for comfort." The couple, who had two sons, Frederick and John Jr., were happy together until John's untimely demise in 1870. With earnings from her writing, Louisa helped Anna purchase the Thoreau House on Main Street in Concord, where Anna lived until her death on July 17, 1893.

BETH

➛ ELIZABETH "LIZZIE" ALCOTT

Of Louisa's sisters, the least is known about Lizzie, who, like Beth, died after contracting scarlet fever months before the Alcotts moved into Orchard House in 1858. What's clear is that her illness took a toll. "A 22-year-old whose disease had wasted her body so that she looked like a middle-aged woman, she lashed out at her family and her fate with an anger that she had never before expressed," Susan Cheever wrote in *Louisa May Alcott: A Personal Biography.* At Lizzie's burial in Concord's Sleepy Hollow Cemetery, Thoreau and Emerson served as pallbearers. "Emerson told the officiating minister, who did not know the family well, that Lizzie was a good, unselfish, patient child, who made friends even in death," John Matteson wrote in *Eden's Outcasts: The Story of Louisa May Alcott and Her Father.* "Everyone seemed to forget that they were not burying a child but a woman of 22."

AMY

➛ ABIGAIL MAY ALCOTT NIERIKER

In *Little Women,* Jo's youngest sister, Amy, aspires to be a great painter; in reality, Louisa's youngest sister, known as May, became a noted visual artist who studied in Boston and in Europe and befriended Impressionist painter Mary Cassatt. "She is a fortunate girl, and always finds some one to help her as she wants to be helped," Louisa wrote in her journal in 1864. In 1877, the Paris Salon accepted one of May's still life paintings. She also wrote a book—*Studying Art Abroad, and How to Do It Cheaply,* offering advice to women who wanted to follow in her footsteps. It was published in 1879, the same year May married Swiss businessman Ernest Nieriker. May died on December 29, 1879, at the age of 39, after giving birth to Louisa May "Lulu" Nieriker. Louisa, then 48, adopted Lulu and brought her home from France to be raised in Massachusetts in accordance with her sister's wishes.

THEODORE "LAURIE" LAURENCE

➛ ALFRED WHITMAN AND LADISLAS WISNIEWSKI

Alcott once wrote in her journal, "Laurie is not an American boy, though every lad I ever knew claims the character." Instead, Alcott says Laurie, Jo's best friend, soul mate, and would-be suitor, was inspired by Ladislas Wisniewski, a young Polish man she met in Switzerland during a vacation to Europe with Boston socialite Anna Weld. Yet experts also believe that Alcott drew certain aspects of Laurie's character from Alfred "Alf" Whitman (left), a fellow member of the Concord Dramatic Union. "She wrote him and said 'You and Laddie,' as she called Wisniewski, 'jointly are Laurie,'" says Alcott scholar Daniel Shealy. "But you get people like [Nathaniel Hawthorne's son] Julian Hawthorne, who claims that Laurie was based on him . . . Julian Hawthorne would claim a lot of things." ●

CHAPTER 2

Great Adaptations

Of the many celluloid and theatrical interpretations of the story—among them PBS's *Masterpiece Theatre* version at right— some have emerged as memorable classics. And as Greta Gerwig's new movie emphatically shows, every generation deserves its own *Little Women*

1933: PURE EXUBERANCE

A FILM STARRING YOUNG KATHARINE HEPBURN STAYED CLOSE TO THE BOOK WHILE ADDING ITS OWN MEASURE OF PLUCK, AND THEN WON AN OSCAR

DIRECTOR GEORGE Cukor's 1933 adaptation of *Little Women* cast a wildly exuberant Katharine Hepburn as Louisa May Alcott's headstrong Jo. And the actress, then 26 years old in just the fourth of what would be nearly four dozen feature film roles, inhabited the part with unbridled gusto.

"Miss Hepburn goes darting through this picture without giving one a moment to think of her as other than Jo," wrote *New York Times* film critic Mordaunt Hall. "It is stimulating to hear Jo sing out: 'Look at me, World, I'm Jo March, and I'm so happy.' She is the personification of sincerity, a thorough human being. Vice is unknown to her, or to the story for that matter."

By the time Cukor's *Little Women* arrived in theaters that November, Alcott's landmark novel already had been translated to the silver screen not once but twice. Two silent versions previously told the tale in both 1917 and 1918. Still, for moviegoers struggling to recover from the sting of the Great Depression, Cukor's film, blessed with the advantage of sound and the unforgettable Hepburn as its winning protagonist, felt like a most welcome surprise.

The retelling is largely faithful to the book: Meg (Frances Dee), Jo (Hepburn), Beth (Jean Parker), and Amy (Joan Bennett) live with their adored mother, Marmee (Spring Byington), in Concord. With the family having fallen on hard times and their father away at war, Meg takes a job as a governess, while Jo cares for the elderly Aunt March (Edna May Oliver) even as she harbors dreams of a writing career. Laurie (Douglass Montgomery) is desperate to marry her, but she rejects his proposal, finding love instead with German émigré Friedrich Bhaer (Paul Lukas), whom she meets in New York.

Cukor (who directed Hepburn in six other films) famously didn't read Alcott's novel before filming, yet he nevertheless captured so much of what makes Alcott's story so beloved—the shared bond among the

DIRECTOR GEORGE CUKOR ON the set of the 1933 film with Katharine Hepburn. Opposite, from left: Hepburn as Jo, Joan Bennett as Amy, Frances Dee as Meg, and Jean Parker as Beth.

sisters, the heartbreak they feel with the death of Beth, the richness and joy they find in life despite their meager circumstances.

"I think for audiences at the time, drowning in the Depression and uncertain about the future, seeing a family successfully pulling together through hard times was difficult to resist," says Kenneth Turan, film critic for the *Los Angeles Times*.

The film became an enormous hit for its studio, RKO, and won an Oscar for its adapted screenplay, which had been written by husband and wife screenwriters Sarah Y. Mason and Victor Heerman. Hepburn was notably influential behind-the-scenes; the actress asked costume designer Walter Plunkett to base one of Jo's ensembles on an old tintype photo of Hepburn's own grandmother.

Despite a performance overflowing with lovable pluck, Hepburn's work in the film was not recognized by the motion picture academy. Still, when it comes to incarnations of New England's wild, rebellious tomboy, hers remains one of the most indelible depictions of Jo ever captured on screen. She transforms the second eldest March sister from a voluble young woman who slides down staircase bannisters and exclaims the name of famous explorers into a complicated, imperfect woman who gains an intimate understanding of the importance of compromise and sacrifice.

"Katharine Hepburn gives an alive and vital portrayal, so convincingly real it delighted audiences back then as much as it does today," Turan says. "Though she'd already won an Oscar [for Best Actress in *Morning Glory*], this was her breakout performance, memorable because it was the template for the on-screen personality that she carried through dozens of films." ●

DOUGLASS MONTGOMERY AS Laurie and Hepburn as Jo engage in playful swordplay, opposite, top. Bottom: In a bit of early merchandising, Madame Alexander created a line of Little Women cloth dolls to coincide with the release of the film; fans could also purchase a set of paper dolls featuring Hepburn's sprightly Jo. This page: The March sisters having a ball.

1949: COLOR BECOMES THEM

YES, THAT WAS ELIZABETH TAYLOR, BLONDE WIG AND ALL, PLAYING THE ROLE OF AMY IN A BEAUTIFULLY COSTUMED TEARJERKER THAT ONCE AGAIN GENERATED ACADEMY AWARD HARDWARE

"G**ET OUT YOUR HAN**-kies, kiddies, and prepare for a nice soggy weep if you go to see 'Little Women,'" wrote critic Bosley Crowther in the March 11, 1949, edition of the *New York Times.* Filmed in glorious Technicolor, Hollywood's second major attempt to adapt Alcott's classic leaned into melodrama, playing the story's maudlin notes the loudest. Still, the movie, directed by Mervyn LeRoy, became a box office sensation.

This time around, 31-year-old June Allyson played 17-year-old Jo, with Janet Leigh as Meg, Margaret O'Brien as Beth, and none other than a teenage Elizabeth Taylor in a blonde wig as Amy. While certain details are different (including a scene where the girls go on a Christmas spending spree), the broad strokes of the story remain the same. Jo is determined to make a name for herself as a writer; Meg marries kindly John Brooke; ambitious Amy weds wealthy Laurie (Peter Lawford) after he is rejected by Jo; and Beth fades away to an untimely death that leaves the family, including Mary Astor's Marmee, heartbroken and bereft.

The idea of remaking *Little Women* had come from the highly successful producer David O. Selznick (*Gone with the Wind*), who had hoped to see his wife, Jennifer Jones, in the starring role. He eventually chose to step away, selling the entirety of the production, including some sets that already had been constructed, to MGM; the studio decided to allow LeRoy to continue on as director.

THE CAST OF THE 1949 FILM, opposite, from left: June Allyson, Margaret O'Brien, Elizabeth Taylor, and Janet Leigh. Here, Allyson (left) and Taylor on set with director Mervyn LeRoy.

Although the film went on to earn an Academy Award for Best Art Direction and Set Decoration, and was also nominated for Best Color Cinematography, critics generally felt that Allyson's portrayal of Jo paled when compared to Hepburn's. Yet for Anne Boyd Rioux, professor of English at the University of New Orleans and the author of 2018's *Meg, Jo, Beth, Amy: The Story of Little Women and Why It Still Matters,* Allyson's Jo is superior.

"To me, she feels more natural," Rioux says. "I think the Katharine Hepburn Jo is overdone. She's very theatrical. Part of that is the era of acting, but I think she overdid the boyish part of it and turned it into a caricature of a tomboy. Jo, she's not putting on an act. She's just being herself, and that self that she is feels more comfortable doing boyish things."

Time magazine, too, had kind things to say of Allyson: "She has a refreshing breeziness and bounce which make the old tale believable and now & then lift it right out of its tatted frame." *Time,* however, did opine that LeRoy had perhaps let his sentimental side get the better of him: "The whole package is so richly wrapped in romantic period sets and costumes that the final shot is unnecessary: a pastel, picture-postcard rainbow rises out of the subsiding suds and sentiments to arch the happy ending."●

LEROY PUT FINISHING touches on Allyson's dress, left. Allyson's Jo and Peter Lawford's Laurie spend time together in Jo's beloved attic sanctuary.

TRY

AUSTRALIAN FILMMAKER Gillian Armstrong on the set of the 1994 film, opposite. Here, Winona Ryder as Jo with Christian Bale as Laurie; Ryder received an Oscar nomination for her performance.

1994: WOMEN IN CHARGE

AN ALL-FEMALE CREATIVE TEAM AND AN EXTRAORDINARY CAST DELIVERED ON A BRAND-NEW SCRIPT THAT BROKE THE *LITTLE WOMEN* MOLD

THE AUSTRALIAN filmmaker Gillian Armstrong knew she had a hit on her hands well before her 1994 adaptation of *Little Women* found its way into theaters. At an early test screening for executives at Columbia Pictures, which had reluctantly agreed to finance the $18 million movie, the sound of sobbing filled the theater as the credits rolled. "That was my best audience screening ever: a room full of men in suits who cried for women," Armstrong told *Vanity Fair* in 2018.

When Armstrong's *Little Women* was released on Christmas Day of 1994, moviegoers came in droves. The movie notably featured an all-women top creative team: director Armstrong, writer Robin Swicord, producer Denise Di Novi, and Amy Pascal, executive vice president of production at Columbia, all of whom cited Alcott's novel as a formative influence. The cast included a who's who of gifted actresses: Winona Ryder starred as Jo, with Trini Alvarado as Meg, Clare Danes (in her first film) as Beth, and, in an unusual twist, Kirsten Dunst playing young Amy and then Samantha Mathis portraying the older Amy.

Future Academy Award winner Christian Bale played the dashing, brooding Laurie; Gabriel Byrne was cast as Jo's future husband, Friedrich Bhaer; and Susan Sarandon gave wise, beloved Marmee a political edge, offering insights such as "Nothing provokes speculation more than the sight of a woman enjoying herself."

"It's certainly a feminist story," Armstrong told *Entertainment Weekly* at the time of the film's release. "In the past movies, they're dewy, girly girls. But actually, they're vain and conceited and love each other, like sisters today."

Rather than attempting a slavish word-for-word adaptation, Swicord wrote the dialogue from scratch to help set the film apart from previous versions. She had spent years thinking about how she would approach the project and how she wanted to bring in

MARMEE (SUSAN SARANDON) reads to Meg (Trini Alvarado), left, Jo, Beth (Claire Danes), and Amy (Kirsten Dunst). Their dresses were created by costume designer Colleen Atwood, who was nominated for an Oscar. Opposite: Jo with future husband Friedrich Bhaer (Gabriel Byrne).

aspects of Alcott's own life, such as her support for women's suffrage, a cause that Jo espouses in the film.

"At some point in my teenage years, I thought, 'I would like to make a movie of *Little Women* because we need one that's not like the other ones,'" Swicord said during an interview in 2019. "The other ones were all about who are these girls going to marry. I knew the book was not about that... I just felt like the politics of that family and her time and who Louisa really was, this sort of subversive way that she was embedding these ideas in her work, I wanted to be able to bring that a little bit more to the surface."

The approach clearly worked. Critics raved. *Variety*'s Todd McCarthy wrote that "1990s audiences are the beneficiaries of an outstanding version of Louisa May Alcott's perennial, one that surpasses even the best previous rendition, George Cukor's 1933 outing starring Katharine Hepburn. A moving, passionately told story about the connections among four generations of a family's women—and, more tellingly, the way women had to struggle to make a mark in a society in which their roles were heavily proscribed—this handsomely produced period piece is easily the most emotionally effective big-screen melodrama since *The Joy Luck Club,* as well as the most intelligent."

The film earned $95 million worldwide, and Winona Ryder was nominated for a Best Actress Oscar for her performance; costume designer Colleen Atwood received her first Academy Award nomination, as did Thomas Newman for his original score (Newman was also nominated that year for *The Shawshank Redemption*). "I don't think anyone really expected it to do as well as it did. It wasn't the talk of the town," Ryder told the *New York Times* in 2019. "It's actually one of the few movies of mine I don't turn off when it comes on because I really like it, and it was such a special experience." ●

2019: THE NEW GENERATION

WITH DIRECTOR GRETA GERWIG LEADING THE WAY, THE NEWEST TELLING OF THE CLASSIC TALE EMBRACES A FRESH TAKE AND A HIGH SPIRIT

EACH GENERATION deserves its own *Little Women.* That was the thinking of producers Amy Pascal, Robin Swicord, and Denise Di Novi when they decided to update Alcott's novel in 2019. It wasn't the first time the Hollywood veterans had teamed up to translate the beloved novel for the screen. Swicord scripted and produced the 1994 version along with Di Novi for Sony Pictures, where Pascal was a high-ranking executive.

Given the richness and depth of the book, the producers felt they could explore different facets of the lives of the Marches with a new film in 2019. "It's a different world now than it was when we made the movie before," says Pascal, who left her post as cochairman of Sony in 2015 to produce full-time. "The thing about the book is that it is much more satirical and knowing and much less sentimental than some of the adaptations have been. And I felt like this was a time where we could do a movie that was truer to the book and truer to Louisa May Alcott."

It was Di Novi who suggested that Greta Gerwig might be the right person for a new adaptation. At the time, Gerwig was best known as an actor whose relatability and charm in such films as director Noah Baumbach's 2010 offbeat comedy, *Greenberg,* had made her a critical darling. She and Baumbach later struck up a writing partnership—Gerwig initially had been interested in a career as a playwright—and their first collaboration, the comedy *Frances Ha,* starred Gerwig as a New York woman who apprentices with a dance company.

"I had loved her as an [actor], but when I saw her screenplay for *Frances Ha,* I thought she had such a specific and deep intimacy with the female experience and a fearlessness in terms of being vulnerable and authentic—that, to me, is what the Jo character embodies," Di Novi says. "Even though it was written at a time when

SAOIRSE RONAN'S JO embraces her inner tomboy as she runs with abandon in the 2019 adaptation. Opposite: Writer-director Greta Gerwig in New York in 2019.

women were so restricted and so constrained, Louisa May Alcott was able to create this character that was so free and so open and did not filter herself, did not diminish herself. I saw that in Greta's work, that fearlessness, that authenticity and the courage to speak your truth."

Gerwig leapt at the opportunity. She had fallen in love with Alcott's novel when she was a girl and felt a kinship with Jo March. "Jo felt like my heroine," Gerwig says. "She was the one I wanted to be like and was like, I suppose, in some ways. She seemed to have stature and that was thrilling."

Gerwig had a specific point of view on the ideas at the heart of Alcott's novel, inspired in part by Virginia Woolf's assertion "Intellectual freedom depends upon material things." "This book is a book about money, and why is it so hard for women to get it," Gerwig says. "The first lines of the book are 'Christmas won't be Christmas without any presents. It's so dreadful to be poor. I don't think it's fair that some girls have lots of pretty things and some girls have nothing at all.' The circumstances of women not being able to earn their own living is everywhere in it.

"Louisa May Alcott, she was one of those people that I think pulled us into the next century," Gerwig adds. "The 20th century was reaching down through her and giving her some ability to say, 'We're going to do this differently moving forward for women.' I don't know that she even understood it completely, but for me that economic piece of being an artist, being a woman, and dealing with money was so much of that entire narrative pulsing underneath the book."

Gerwig also felt strongly about how the sisters should be depicted. Specifically, she was interested in changing the perception of Amy from the pampered diva of the March clan—a girl more concerned with the shape of her nose than with the more serious interests of her sisters—into an assertive woman unafraid to pursue what she wanted from life. "I wanted her to be a worthy adversary for Jo," Gerwig says. "She and Jo are the two that have the biggest, brightest, craziest ambition. She has her eye on the door the whole time the way Jo does. She even has a line in the book, 'The world is hard on ambitious girls.' Often, Amy is played as being a bit prissy, and she's anything but. She's

a monster. She wants to be the best artist in the world. That part of Amy is the same as Jo."

Pascal and the other producers were impressed by Gerwig's fresh perspective and the passion with which she articulated her ideas. In 2014, they hired her to adapt the screenplay. "[We realized] that there was probably nobody else who could tell the story the way that she could," Pascal says.

It wasn't the only script Gerwig was writing at the time. She'd also been working on *Lady Bird,* a coming-of-age tale set in Sacramento about a Catholic high school student desperate to break out of her lower-middle-class suburban life. For the story, Gerwig borrowed elements from her own life. She, too, had grown up in the California capital, attending an all-girls Catholic school and longing to find a creative outlet.

The Irish actor Saoirse Ronan starred as Christine "Lady Bird" McPherson, a teen who has a difficult relationship with her mother, Marion (Laurie Metcalf), finds herself floundering in her friendship with bestie Julie (Beanie Feldstein), and meets an effortlessly cool but ultimately useless boy named Kyle, played by Timothée Chalamet, who briefly claims Lady Bird's affections but breaks her heart.

The film opened in 2017 to rapturous reviews and went on to earn five Academy Award nominations; Gerwig became only the fifth woman nominated for Best Director. *Lady Bird* further proved to *Little Women*'s producing team that no one but Gerwig should direct their film. Her understanding of the complexities of female

AMY (FLORENCE PUGH) burns Jo's manuscript in a fit of rage, opposite. Above: Beth (Eliza Scanlen) arranges a bouquet of wildflowers.

relationships, the sympathy with which she treats her characters, and the humor with which she approaches the absurdities of life all made her, in the producers' view, exactly the right filmmaker to bring Alcott's classic to the screen.

"She's got it all," Pascal says. "She's incredibly sophisticated about the way that she shoots. She's a brilliant writer, and the way that she works with actors is like the best of them. She gets right inside the characters. She brings things out in people. She's incredibly patient. She knows exactly what she wants, and she had a vision for this movie that was completely her own."

It was clear from the start that Gerwig would reteam with her *Lady Bird* stars Ronan and Chalamet in the roles of Jo and Laurie. "We never really thought of anybody else except for Saoirse and Timothée to play those characters," Pascal says. "It just seemed obvious, not only because of their relationship on that movie but also who they are in the world, what wonderful actors they are, and how much we felt they could break each other's hearts."

Gerwig says that, for her, Ronan was as much a creative partner as an actor playing a role. "I said this when we made *Lady Bird* together, and it's true of this one, too. She's the cocreator of these films in the sense that she's an author. It's not just that she's saying things I've written; she really creates what the thing is. I don't know any other way to describe it. Like all great actors, she's a great filmmaker."

The rest of the cast is no less impressive. Emma Watson was brought on to play Meg March alongside talented newcomers Eliza Scanlen and Florence Pugh, chosen for Beth and Amy, respectively. Laura Dern agreed to play Marmee; Bob Odenkirk, Father March; and Chris Cooper, Laurie's grandfather, Mr. Laurence. And Meryl Streep signed on to play Aunt March, the opinionated wealthy relative who has no compunction about sharing her feelings about the family of troublemakers.

EMMA WATSON AS MEG, Pugh as Amy, Ronan as Jo, and Scanlen as Beth.

MERYL STREEP, AS THE sisters' wealthy, difficult Aunt March. Opposite: Fast friends Jo (Ronan) and Laurie (Timothée Chalamet)

That such an ensemble would team up for the film is a testament to the source material and to Gerwig's reputation, according to Swicord. "Her deep acting background gives her the confidence to let actors take the lead and be messy and try things," she says. "There's a wrong idea that many directors have—somehow they're in control and they're kind of a puppeteer, and it's their job to get the actors to do things a certain way to match a sort of preimagined performance. Greta has tremendous strength as a director because she fearlessly lets actors do human behavior and find things. She knows how to encourage them, and at the same time, how to begin to shape their performance."

WRITERS HAVE AN EAR FOR LANguage in the way composers have an ear for the rhythms of sound. As Gerwig wrote the *Little Women* script, she realized that there was no better source for the words to tell the story than the author herself. Gerwig returned to the novel time and again to find dialogue for her characters, in addition to using comments and observations taken from Alcott's letters to and from her loved ones. "I tried to use as much actual language from the book as possible," Gerwig says. "Every line in the movie is either from the book or from a letter or a journal. I wanted everything to be grounded in something I could point to."

Hearing the words spoken aloud, Gerwig was struck by how contemporary the speech sounded. "I had always had this idea of the cacophony of when they were young, how loud it was with four girls in one house," she says. "I wanted that very tight talking over each other to sound like a musical without music in a way. They're so famous, some of these lines. They're like Shakespeare in terms of being lodged in common memory. Saying them fast and casual and one on top of

Excerpted from *Little Women: The Official Movie Companion* by Gina McIntyre. © 2019 Columbia Pictures Industries, Inc. Published by arrangement with Abrams Books for Young Readers, an imprint of ABRAMS. All Rights Reserved.

FROM LEFT TO RIGHT: Pugh as Amy, Ronan as Jo, and Watson as Meg.

the other took away the preciousness. It made it so it didn't feel like every line had been embroidered on a pillow."

Gerwig did diverge from the source material in one vitally important way: Alcott's novel proceeds chronologically, beginning with the girls in adolescence and moving forward into their adult years. Gerwig's screenplay does not. She wanted to emphasize the March sisters as young women in the world, with flashbacks to the past playing out in a way that would have the soft, hazy glow of memory. The approach allowed her to explore different aspects of the sisters' lives and the struggles they face in their later years.

"What I had found so fascinating about the book when I was reading it as an adult were the parts where they're dealing with adulthood," Gerwig says. "Meg has twins, and she's trapped in a cottage with these twins all day. She's losing her mind and then she spends too much money on credit that she doesn't have. The matrimonial discord around that could have been written yesterday."

"I wanted to put more emphasis on them as young adults, and make what was magical about their childhood feel almost bittersweet and achy because it's somehow gone," she says. "I wanted to give these characters a path to adulthood and keep what was special and unique and sort of irrepressible about who they were as children."

Gerwig was also struck by the hardships that Alcott faced and how she nevertheless managed to create a fictionalized family that felt perfect in so many ways. "I found the tension between the content of the book and the content of Louisa May Alcott's life really interesting," Gerwig says. "That break between what was, in many ways, a very unhappy childhood, then turning that into something that's seen as an idyllic childhood is, for me, fascinating as someone who writes. It's also heartbreaking. She has a quote: 'I have had lots of troubles, so I write jolly tales,' which just about makes me want to cry. She had a lot of sadness, but through that misfortune, she knew how to describe this idyllic childhood." ●

LIGHTS, CAMERAS, AND SO MUCH ACTION

BEYOND THE DEFINITIVE VERSIONS, LITTLE WOMEN HAS BEEN TRANSLATED TO THE SCREEN TIME AND AGAIN ACROSS MANY DECADES—AND NATIONS

IN THE ROUGHLY 150 YEARS since it was first published, *Little Women* has been translated into more than 50 languages and has inspired numerous film and television adaptations. There's a simple reason that Alcott's novel is updated so often, according to television critic Maureen Ryan: Its themes and its characters are always relevant to young audiences. "There are certain coming-of-age stories that just really resonate with people," Ryan says. "Before there was Harry Potter and being able to sort yourself into a different house, there was 'Which March sister are you?' Now, there's a massive explosion of YA fiction or YA TV shows—that didn't exist when I was growing up. But *Little Women* was always there. It was something you could [revisit] again and again and again."

Following is a roundup of some of the most notable versions to appear on screens big and small.

LITTLE WOMEN (1918)

This silent 60-minute version starred Dorothy Bernard as Jo and was shot in Concord, Massachusetts. The previous year a British silent film starring Ruby Miller as Jo was released, but it is now believed to be lost.

LITTLE MEN (1940, 1998)

In 1940, RKO released a streamlined adaptation of Alcott's novel about life at the Plumfield Farm Boarding School that deviated substantially

LITTLE WOMEN GETS THE silent treatment in a 1918 film, opposite, directed by Harley Knoles and starring, from left, Henry Hull, Lillian Hall, Dorothy Bernard, and Conrad Nagel. Here: Cast members of the 1950–1951 BBC production included Norah Gorsen as Beth, at the piano, with Jane Hardie as Jo (left), Susan Stephen as Amy, and Sheila Shand Gibbs as Meg.

from the source material. In a review, *Time* magazine described the film as "a period piece as heavy as a Victorian sideboard." A 1998 television series also adapted *Little Men,* with Michelle Burke playing Jo Bhaer. That same year, a feature film directed by Rodney Gibbons and starring Mariel Hemingway as Jo also arrived onscreen.

LITTLE WOMEN (1950)

The BBC broadcast an adaptation of a play based on the book. Written by Winifred Oughton and Brenda R. Thompson, the six-episode miniseries became notable for being the most complete adaptation then attempted.

LITTLE WOMEN (1958)

Richard Adler of *Damn Yankees* fame wrote music and lyrics for the eight songs featured in this one-hour musical adaptation, which was written by Wilson Lehr and aired on CBS. Florence Henderson (who later starred as Carol Brady in *The Brady Bunch*) played Meg, while Margaret O'Brien reprised her role of Beth from the 1949 film, though her character's death was omitted from the production. The cast recording is still available—and features a young Joel Grey as Laurie.

LITTLE WOMEN (1970)

The BBC again staged Alcott's tale, this time as a nine-part miniseries, but results were mixed—it was hampered by poor production values and the English cast struggled to affect American accents.

LITTLE WOMEN (1978)

NBC aired a two-part adaptation notable for, among other things, having *Star Trek* icon William Shatner in the role of Professor Bhaer. *The Partridge Family's* Susan Dey played Jo; Meredith Baxter Birney was Meg; Eve Plumb (also of *The Brady Bunch*) was Beth; and Ann Dusenberry was Amy. It won Emmy Awards for art direction and cinematography.

WILLIAM SHATNER'S Friedrich Bhaer confesses his feelings for Susan Dey's Jo in NBC's 1978 miniseries.

MR. LAURENCE (MICHAEL Gambon) shares a dance with Aunt March (Angela Lansbury) in 2018's adaptation of *Little Women* that aired on PBS.

FOUR SISTERS OF YOUNG GRASS (1981)

In Japan, *Little Women* is one of most widely read books among girls. This 26-episode anime series, titled *Wakakusa no Yon Shimai,* was based on an animated TV special that adapted Alcott's book. Anne Boyd Rioux, professor of English at the University of New Orleans and the author of 2018's *Meg, Jo, Beth, Amy: The Story of Little Women and Why It Still Matters,* adores the translation of the title: "It's a metaphor for coming of age, growing up."

LOVE'S TALE OF YOUNG GRASS (1987)

A second anime version of *Little Women, Ai no Wakakusa Monogatari,* strayed much further from the original text, adding new characters to Alcott's story. In 1988, a version that had been dubbed into English ran on HBO under the title *Tales of Little Women.*

LITTLE WOMEN (2018)

A three-part retelling from the BBC that aired on PBS's *Masterpiece Theatre* earned high marks for winning performances from a gifted cast led by Maya Hawke, in her first onscreen role, as Jo. The production also featured Willa Fitzgerald as Meg, Annes Elwy as Beth, Kathryn Newton as Amy, Emily Watson as Marmee, Jonah Hauer-King as Laurie, Dylan Baker as Mr. March—and Angela Lansbury as Aunt March. The opportunity was a singular one for Hawke, who dropped out of Juilliard to play Jo, whom she had long considered her "hero." "She's like her sisters in that they're all striving to be their best self—they're all fundamentally honest and loving towards each other—and she's different in that she is not satisfied with her current circumstances," Hawke said in an interview at the time of the program's release. "She's not satisfied with the amount of education she's been allowed to have, with the clothes she has to wear, with the place she lives. She wants more from life. I think that's something people connect to, and I think that's what makes her really individual." ●

UNPEELING THE OPERA

THE HIGHLY SUCCESSFUL OPERA OF *LITTLE WOMEN* OWES ITS PASSION TO ITS CREATOR, MARK ADAMO, WHO EXPLAINS HERE WHAT MAKES THIS ADAPTATION SING

WHEN THE IDEA of a *Little Women* opera was proposed to Mark Adamo in 1996 as a commission, the then fledgling composer didn't spark to the idea. But once he revisited Louisa May Alcott's novel, and his own childhood, he was able to locate a truth in the March sisters' bond, one that felt very much like that shared by Adamo's own siblings. He also homed in on what he felt was the central struggle for the upstart heroine, Jo: her desire for the status quo of her loving home to remain unchanged. "As Meg and Laurie awaken sexually, and Beth accepts death, they each move away from this idyll of childhood friendship in which Jo—herself half a child—has thrived for so long," Adamo says. "Suddenly it occurred to me that if anyone—young or old, female or male—had ever either heard, or uttered, the words, 'I think I've outgrown this relationship,' that *Little Women* was the story of your life."

LIFE recently spoke with Adamo about his opera, which has enjoyed a long and successful life since it was first produced at the Houston Grand Opera in 1998. A full-scale staging from 2000 yielded a PBS *Great Performances* broadcast and a two-CD set on the Ondine label. More than a dozen companies across the country have mounted subsequent productions of the two-act work, making it one of the most frequently performed American operas of its time.

Had you ever planned to write an opera before the Summer Opera came to you with the commission?
Yes and no. I had trained as a composer and librettist for the theatre, but the musicals I most admired aspired to the condition of opera: Sondheim's *Sweeney Todd,* Bernstein's *Candide,* Loesser's Most *Happy Fella,* for example. And the operas I most admired incorporated elements of the musical theatre: Gershwin's *Porgy and Bess,* or Menotti's *The Consul.*

What was your reaction to their proposal?
I was ambivalent. I'd read the book as a young boy—say, eight years old—at the same time my two older sisters, who were 11 and 12 years old, had read it, and I remember being very moved by it. But it seemed to be more a collection of short stories [rather] than a conflict-driven novel. So, I reread the novel, but also researched every film and theatrical adaptation I could find. At that point, I could locate three American film versions, a television series, a Japanese anime adaptation, and three attempts for the theater. None of which, to me, worked.

What was the key to understanding how to get the adaptation right?
First, I tried to avoid the mistakes many others made. The earliest adaptations focused, at first, on the relationships among the sisters but then inevitably bent over backward trying to make them into the heroines of conventional romances, which, in Alcott's book, they are emphatically not. Later, more overtly feminist versions, like Gillian Armstrong's film from 1994, took Jo's artistic ambitions seriously, but made her more conventionally feminine, and more of a victim . . . than Alcott did.

The important mistakes people made, I think, were two. The first was

ignoring what we would now call the Alcotts'/Marches' privilege. Both the historical Alcotts and *Little Women*'s fictionalized version of them weren't poor. They were rich members of the progressive Boston intelligentsia who'd lost most of their money, which is a distinction with a difference. As such, they can seem weirdly modern. For example, Jo, at 19, writes her first novel, which is not thrown on the trash heap because it was written by a young woman but is reviewed promptly and seriously, if not unanimously, by serious critics of the day. Jo, confused by the lack of critical consensus, complains to her mother, who utters the 19th-century equivalent of "You can't trust the *Boston Globe*." Whatever else that chapter is, it's not a story of a young woman artist silenced by the patriarchy.

The second mistake was not taking the emotional bonds among the sisters very seriously. I grew up with two sisters and saw how intense female bonding could be. Everywhere in the first part of the book there are clues that Jo has with her sisters—and knows she has—the balance of emotional support and personal freedom that we moderns seek, and rarely find, in marriage. What links the important episodes of [the story]—Meg's marriage

CAST MEMBERS OF NEW YORK City Opera's production of Mark Adamo's *Little Women* performed in Tokyo in 2005.

to Brooke, Laurie's infatuation with Jo, Beth's death—is that each of these characters, in growing up, abandons Jo in some way.

Little Women became an immediate hit when it was staged at the Houston Grand Opera. Were you surprised?
Yes and no. We had an extraordinary creative team, and it was clear in rehearsal that we had something special. But after the last bars of the first performance, we did have that very special long silence that happens when audiences don't want to break the spell. That was my first clue that we wouldn't hear the last of this piece.

The opera has enjoyed longevity and enduring popularity. Why do you think that is?
As of 2020, the number of separate productions is 133. It's been done four to seven times a year, every year, since 1998. In 2016, it was produced 12 times. The appeal of the book is one reason the opera's endured, and the music has been warmly received. As a dramatist, though, I did my best to make the opera's title characters modern American women like the ones Alcott wrote and the ones I know, with thoughts as well as feelings and a full range of the latter—anger as well as patience, ambition as well as love.

Why do you think Alcott's work still resonates so strongly, and not just on the page, but also in film, television, and on the stage?
It was only about 20 years ago that more scholars started to afford the book the respect routinely granted to, say, *Tom Sawyer* or *Huckleberry Finn*. And yet, American cultural products ranging from Mary McCarthy's *The Group* through *Sex and the City* to Lena Dunham's *Girls* are unimaginable without the template Alcott forged. In each, a small, highly various group of sisters—or friends who relate like sisters—use their closeness and conflicts to explore what it is to be a woman today. ●

NATE MANN AND KRISTOLYN Lloyd during a May 2019 rehearsal of *Little Women* at New York's Cherry Lane Theater, above. Here: Maureen McGovern, center, as Marmee, and, clockwise from bottom left, Megan McGinnis as Beth, Amy McAlexander as Amy, Jenny Powers as Meg, and Sutton Foster as Jo in a performance of the 2005 Broadway musical.

ON BROADWAY, AND OFF

Recent stage adaptations have produced some memorable performances, as well as a powerful version for these times

THE FIRST TIME *LITTLE Women* came to Broadway, it was a hit 1912 production adapted by Marian de Forest and created by American theater director and actress Jessie Bonstelle. Roughly four decades later, two Broadway musicals, both titled *Jo,* attempted to translate Alcott's tale. And about four decades after that, in 2005, *Little Women* returned to Broadway as a high-profile musical with a score by Jason Howland, lyrics by Mindi Dickstein and book by Allan Knee. Susan H. Schulman directed and *Thoroughly Modern Millie* star Sutton Foster played Jo, with Broadway vet Maureen McGovern as Marmee.

"I honestly feel like I'm most one with Jo," Foster said before the play opened. "Like Jo, I was always inviting friends over and writing scripts and making them act in these sort of murder-mystery plays, whether they wanted to or not. Jo's an incredible character to play. It's been really fun getting to know her more and more—because every night you perform it, you learn more and more about the part you're playing."

Foster received glowing reviews and was nominated for a Tony Award for her performance—which included belting out the show-stopping number "Astonishing." Yet critics felt that the musical itself didn't quite capture the magic of the original text. "Watching this shorthand account of four sisters growing up poor but honest during the Civil War is like speed reading Alcott's evergreen novel of 1868," Ben Brantley wrote in the *New York Times.* "You glean the most salient traits of the principal characters, events and moral lessons, but without the shading and detail that made these elements feel true to life in the book."

•••

The most recent stage production of *Little Women* debuted at Minneapolis's Jungle Theater in 2018 with nonbinary actor C. Michael Menge in the lead as Jo.

Playwright Kate Hamill already had tackled classics such as *Sense and Sensibility, Vanity Fair* and *Pride and Prejudice* when she her sights on Alcott, updating the works through what she describes as a "radical feminist lens."

"I was really interested in doing a story about American women—because it is a quintessentially American story—and how to reconcile the dictates of your own conscience with what society expects of you," says Hamill, who also played Meg in the production. She also wanted to create a play that was intentionally inclusive—stagings are required to cast actors of color in its principal roles. "I was particularly interested in creating a version that let LGBTQ teenagers understand that they've always been a part of history, they've always been a part of American stories. My Jo is pretty explicitly not straight . . . I just felt like we don't really need another heteronormative love story."

Although Kristolyn Lloyd took over the role of Jo opposite Hamill's Meg when the production, directed by Sarna Lapine, opened off Broadway in June 2019, critics noted that many of its most modern ideas about gender remained intact. Wrote Laura Collins-Hughes in her review for the *New York Times:* "'You can be lonely in a crowd, if it's not the right crowd,' Jo tells the girls, and so she is, stuck in a world of women when her every fiber yearns to adventure alongside the men. All the nonsense restrictions of ladylike behavior—and feminine dress—only make her struggle harder."

And, as Hamill notes, *Little Women* is in part "about people trying to live their lives and figure out who they are against the backdrop of this huge systemic overturn [of the Civil War]. I feel like that is pretty relatable. I think we're always trying to figure out the arcs of ourselves against the arcs of human history." ●

CHAPTER 3

A Lasting Legacy

The desk, at right, from which Louisa May Alcott moved heaven and earth continues to draw visitors from across the globe, while the lessons and attitudes championed by *Little Women* have influenced a range of notable thinkers, J.K. Rowling and Joey Tribbiani among them

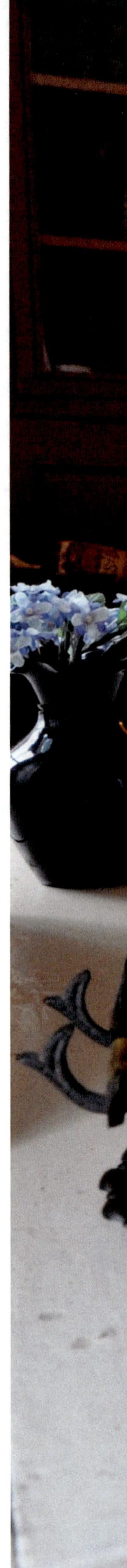

A SPECIAL PLACE

THE HOME AND LAND WHERE THE ALCOTTS LIVED, AND WHERE LOUISA WROTE, REMAINS LARGELY INTACT—PROVIDING A FAMILIAR AMBIENCE FOR ANYONE WHO KNOWS *LITTLE WOMEN*

SITUATED ON 12 ACRES amid dozens of apple trees, Orchard House is forever memorialized in *Little Women* as the loving home where the March sisters dwell. And it still exists, preserved as a time capsule of late-19th-century American life. The historic property in Concord, Massachusetts, is open to the public and each year hosts thousands of guests coming to see the home where Louisa May Alcott lived and wrote her most famous tale.

"The wandering family is anchored at last," Alcott said after her clan was finally settled in Orchard House in 1858. That, however, took some time. When Bronson Alcott purchased Orchard House the previous year, the structures that stood on the land dated to the 1660s and were in terrible disrepair. Many people assumed they would be torn down and the lumber used for firewood. Instead, Bronson set about refurbishing the buildings.

The decision was in part practical—he couldn't afford to pay for demolition and new construction—but he also wanted to salvage a piece of the past. "He appreciated the history—he really was a preservationist of sorts," says Jan

ORCHARD HOUSE, LOUISA MAY Alcott's childhood home and the setting for her novel *Little Women*, in Concord, Massachusetts, as photographed in 2009.

Turnquist, executive director of the Orchard House museum. "He and carpenters worked on the external things, and his daughters painted and papered inside. It was a big family effort."

The Alcotts moved into Orchard House in 1858, just after the death of Louisa's sister Lizzie, and lived there until 1877 (the home was eventually sold to prominent transcendentalist William Torrey Harris). Bronson hosted his close friends Henry David Thoreau and Ralph Waldo Emerson in the study; Anna Alcott wed John Pratt in the parlor; and of course, Louisa, seated at the desk her father had built for her, wrote *Little Women*.

Of the many treasures preserved at the museum, the following are just a few of the highlights that might feel familiar to those whose lives have been touched by *Little Women*.

SCHOOL OF PHILOSOPHY AND LITERATURE

To the left of Orchard House is a barnlike structure that was home to Bronson Alcott's adult education program, the Concord School of Philosophy and Literature. "It was built as a small lecture hall," Turnquist says. "He wanted a vaulted ceiling so that it would almost feel chapel-like. A lot of transcendental philosophy took place in that building and transcendentalism is a very spiritual philosophy."

The building is not open to visitors, but you can glimpse the interior in the 2019 *Little Women* film: The building doubles as the school where young Amy (Florence Pugh) finds herself in trouble after drawing an unflattering portrait of her instructor.

THE PARLOR

The receiving area for guests would be transformed when it was time for the Alcott sisters to put on performances of their own invention as entertainment. "They would have their audience sit in the parlor, and between the parlor and the dining room, they'd put up a curtain—the dining room was really their stage and the audience would sit in the parlor,"

THE HEART OF ORCHARD House was the parlor, foreground, and the dining room. The doors between the rooms would be removed when the Alcott sisters performed plays for guests seated in the parlor. The door to the kitchen also can be seen, as well as the staircase (at right) leading to May's bedchamber.

Turnquist says. "They'd be able to close the curtain between acts, run up the back stairs to May's bedchamber and come back down and continue the play. They did very elaborate plays, with lots of costumes and props. They spent hours putting these things together. When they performed, it was quite a production!"

LIZZIE'S MELODEON

Although Lizzie died before the Alcotts could move into Orchard House, the small organ that belonged to Louisa's sister was an important memory of the family's lost daughter who was thought of as the "angel in the house." The Alcotts "all were quite musical actually, but [Lizzie] was the one who was really passionate about music," Turnquist says. "She did get a piano. The melodeon is what she had at first, but it's very hard to play because it's like a little organ. You have to pump a bellows to get the sound out . . . The melodeon . . . was just precious to them as a reminder of her."

BRONSON ALCOTT'S STUDY

A focal point of the house, the study looks today just as it did when Emerson and Thoreau spent time there. "The carpet on the floor and the wallpaper on the walls in that room are precisely what was in there when May Alcott helped redecorate after Louisa had made money from *Little Women,*" Turnquist says. One key addition, though, is a bust of Bronson completed after his death by acclaimed sculptor Daniel Chester French (who most famously designed the statue of Abraham Lincoln that sits in the Lincoln Memorial).

MAY'S ARTWORK

Visitors to Orchard House will see many sketches created by May when she was a child, some of which are painted directly

THE KITCHEN AT ORCHARD House, top left; the melodeon in the parlor, top right; Bronson Alcott's study, right.

ONE OF MAY ALCOTT'S EARLY drawings, titled "Aurora Greeting the Dawn," top left; Anna's wedding dress was made from gray silk, left; Louisa's writing desk, built by Bronson Alcott, was the focal point of her bedroom, right.

onto her bedroom walls. "It's a testament to their charm that nobody ever felt the need to paint over those sketches," Turnquist says. "The drawings are for some people the most memorable part of the entire house." May also was excited to explore other media, including pyrography, in which designs are burned into wood to create decorations.

Just like Amy March, the character she inspired, May was also interested in working in plaster. In *Little Women,* Amy tries to cast her foot from plaster. "May Alcott had done this," Turnquist says. "She tries plaster molding and thinks well, I'll put my foot in a bucket of plaster and I'll get a mold. She didn't realize that when the plaster dried, she'd have a bucket stuck on her foot."

ANNA'S WEDDING GOWN

In *Little Women,* Meg March's wedding to John Brooke is a turning point for Jo, who sulks. "I just wish I could marry Meg myself, and keep her safe in the family." Meg's nuptials were based on the wedding of Louisa's sister Anna, who took her vows in the family home. The handmade dress she wore is displayed each year at the end of May, the time of Anna's anniversary.

"It's made of gray silk," Turnquist says. "You could be married in any color—it was just whatever color you liked for your best dress. Clearly, it was a treasured best dress that she took wonderful care of after the wedding, too, because it's beautifully preserved. It was not worn for just any old event after the wedding. In general, the trend that you see now, to have a wedding dress for that day and then it's never worn again, was not very much in vogue then. Anna treasured this dress."

LOUISA'S WRITING DESK

"For women, it was considered improper to write for the public. If you did, you were a little too cutting-edge for most people," Turnquist says. "Louisa and her family were always a little too cutting-edge for a lot of people." Although her desk is small by today's standards, the fact that it existed was remarkable given societal norms. "[People thought that] brainwork would destroy your health if you were a woman," Turnquist says. "But Bronson Alcott could see that his daughter was passionate about this—he did not agree with the prevailing wisdom, he just wanted to encourage her. Today, people look at it and think, It's so small! But it was hers. And it was dedicated to her writing and it was placed in a wonderful location where she could look out." ●

AS A YOUNG GIRL AND AN aspiring author, J.K. Rowling took encouragement from Alcott's heroine Jo March. French writer Simone de Beauvoir, opposite, at her home in Paris in 1949, is one of the many preeminent thinkers who have cited Alcott's work as a primary influence.

ACTIVIST GLORIA STEINEM, top left, photographed in New York City in 2015, numbers among Alcott's famous fans, as does music legend Patti Smith, top right, who made mention of reading *Little Women* in her youth in her 2010 memoir *Just Kids*. U.S. poet laureate Tracy K. Smith, right, has said that "*Little Women* made me into a reader."

FORMER SECRETARY OF STATE Hillary Clinton, opposite, right, in Washington, D.C., in 2018, and former First Lady Laura Bush, pictured in the White House library in 2002, have both praised *Little Women*, as did President Theodore Roosevelt (here), who was also partial to Alcott's sequel, *Little Men*.

and her most widely beloved character.

"Jo does not fly in the face of tradition in an offensive way," Turnquist says. "She leads one to think, how can you be your own independent spirit even if what you're doing doesn't fit someone else's idea of what you should do? At the same time, Jo cares about her family. She's trying to face her own demons, her temper, but she also recognizes that she is who she is, so she doesn't completely fall apart when she fails. She dusts herself off and tries again, which is very admirable, and I think that's a great example."

FOR WRITERS THE EXAMPLE OF the book, and Jo, can be particularly resonant. In 1994, Ann Petry, who became the first African American writer to sell more than a million copies with her 1946 Harlem-set novel *The Street,* singled out Jo March as a formative influence. "I couldn't stop reading because I had encountered Jo March," Petry said when she was inducted into the Connecticut Women's Hall of Fame. "I felt as though I was part of Jo and she was part of me. I too, was a tomboy and a misfit and kept a secret diary... She said things like 'I wish I was a horse, then I could run for miles in the splendid air and not lose my breath.' I found myself wishing the same thing whenever I ran for the sheer joy of running. She was a would-be writer and so was I."

The prolific author Cynthia Ozick wrote in a 1982 essay that she read *Little Women* "a thousand times. Ten thousand. I am no longer incognito, not even myself. I am Jo in her 'vortex'; not Jo exactly but some Jo-of-the-future. I am under an enchantment: Who I truly am must be deferred, waited for and waited for."

The list truly goes on and on. YA favorite John Green (*The Fault in Our Stars*) has said *Little Women* ranks among his literary influences and he "didn't understand why boys weren't supposed to read [the novel]." In 2018, Peruvian-American author Natalia Sylvester (*Everyone Knows You Go Home*) selected *Little Women* as one of the three books that changed the course of her life, "By the time I was 12 I was obsessed," she said in an interview with the website GirlBoss. "I followed Jo's life with the fervor of a child reading an adventure book. Her constant push to live life on her terms was heroic to me."

Patti Smith, the singer-songwriter who was an early icon of the New York City punk rock movement, wrote of her love for the book in a 2018 essay for the *Paris Review.* "I drew comfort from my books," Smith wrote. "Oddly enough, it was Louisa May Alcott who provided me with a positive view of my female destiny. Jo, the tomboy of the four March sisters in *Little Women,* writes to help support her family, struggling to make ends meet during the Civil War. She fills page after page with her rebellious scrawl, later published in the literary pages of her local newspaper. She gave me the courage of a new goal, and soon I was crafting little stories and spinning long yarns for my brother and sister. From that time on, I cherished the idea that one day I would write a book." ●

POP CULTURE POWERHOUSE

A PLOTLINE IN *FRIENDS*. A POINT OF CONFLICT IN *GIRLS*. A RUN OF NEW LITERARY INTERPRETATIONS. *LITTLE WOMEN* IS WORKING IT

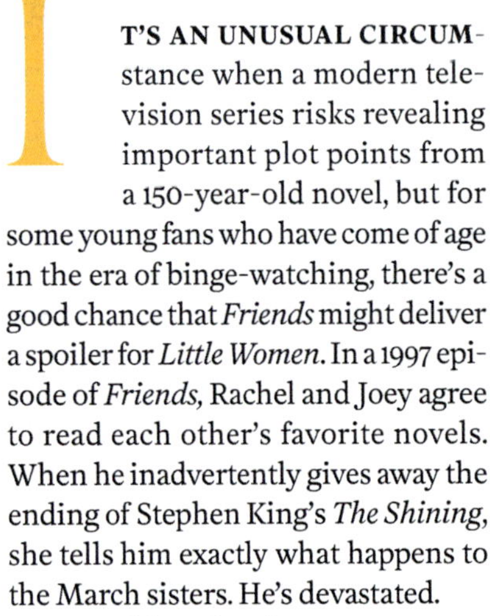

IT'S AN UNUSUAL CIRCUMstance when a modern television series risks revealing important plot points from a 150-year-old novel, but for some young fans who have come of age in the era of binge-watching, there's a good chance that *Friends* might deliver a spoiler for *Little Women*. In a 1997 episode of *Friends*, Rachel and Joey agree to read each other's favorite novels. When he inadvertently gives away the ending of Stephen King's *The Shining*, she tells him exactly what happens to the March sisters. He's devastated.

"I would say that the current generation of young people watching *Friends* is less likely to understand the *Little Women* reference than the generation that watched it when [the show] first came out," says Beverly Lyon Clark, author of 2015's *The Afterlife of Little Women* and the editor of *Louisa May Alcott: The Contemporary Reviews*. "The percentage of people who read the book when young is not as high as it once was."

Given *Little Women*'s ongoing presence in so many avenues of popular culture, one doesn't necessarily have to have read the book to know the highlights of the story. From passing references in TV shows to commercial fiction (and some weightier literary endeavors), *Little Women* is thriving in the modern imagination.

Friends wasn't the first hit TV series to deploy an Alcott-inspired story line. In 1977, an episode of *Little House on the Prairie* titled "Little Women" sees shy Ginny Clark learn valuable lessons while playing the part of Jo in a school production. More recently, the costume drama *Downton Abbey* cited Alcott's novel when Cora Crawley complained to her lady's maid, "No one ever warns you about bringing up daughters. You think it's going to be like *Little Women*. Instead they're at each other's throats from dawn until dusk."

There are contemporary examples, too. The second season of the HBO comedy *Girls* features an extended side plot in which Ray attempts to get Lena Dunham's aspiring writer Hannah to return his copy of *Little Women*, a gift from his grandmother. The connection between Alcott and the acclaimed series Dunham created—about four young women trying to find their way as young adults in New York—has been noted many times over; in 2013, Chiara Atik fused the two for her play *Women*.

"Alcott's wholesome 1868 novel is the O.G. when it comes to quartets of girls figuring it all out," Atik wrote in a 2014 essay on Vulture, "*Girls* and *Little Women*: How Hannah Horvath Is Like Jo March." "*Little Women* and *Girls* share the same plot, give or take a sex scene or two; they both tell the story of four girls trying (to varying degrees of success) to grow up."

In her 2018 novel, *The Spring Girls*, Anna Todd also put a modern spin on *Little Women*. Beverly Lyon Clark

WRITTEN BY REY TERCIERO and illustrated by Bre Indigo, *Meg, Jo, Beth, and Amy: A Graphic Novel: A Modern Retelling of Little Women*, opposite, contemporizes Alcott's classic and sees Jo come out as gay by the story's end. Above: The Japanese publisher Kodansha released its own *Little Women* book series.

I HOPE I FIND MY PRINCE.
I HOPE I FIND TRUE LOVE.
ALL OF YOU WILL.
WHY DO HAPPY MOVIES MAKE US CRY?
I'M NOT CRYING.
SNIFF
NOT REALLY.
SNIFF
OKAY, MAYBE JUST A LITTLE.

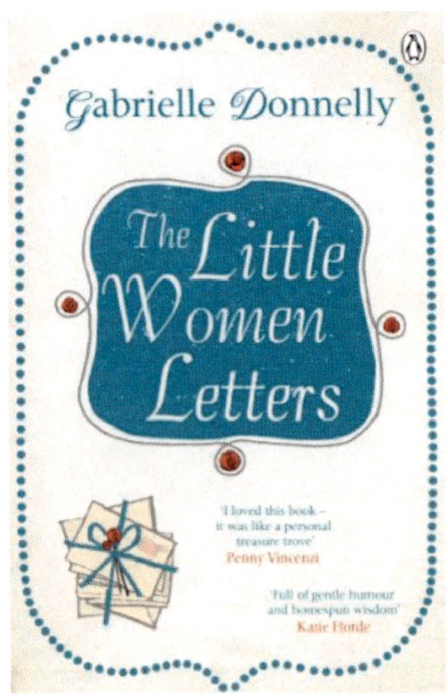

describes Todd's Meg, Jo, Beth, and Amy as "lusty little women." The update is set on a New Orleans military base, with the sisters' father deployed to Iraq. Long before she ever set out to write the book, Todd had been an admirer of the classic text. "I was fascinated by this idea of having four girls living in one house going through the same things together, and [I was drawn to] Jo's personality," she says. "She had so much confidence and was so smart and wasn't embarrassed by how eccentric she was."

With one caveat: Todd was incensed that Jo did not end up with Laurie. So, in *The Spring Girls,* she rewrites that story line. "I've been pissed for 15 years," Todd says. "I really do understand why [Alcott made that choice], but I just couldn't live with it. I didn't like the professor. He's very grumpy and makes [Jo] feel small for writing what she wants to write. I felt like, even if it wasn't Laurie, why did she end up with this not-great guy when she's one of the best female characters ever written? And then to have Laurie marry Jo's sister, I was like, this isn't fair! I redid that immediately."

The temptation to imagine alternate narratives involving Alcott's beloved characters has proved alluring. In her 2010 book, *The Little Women Letters,* Gabrielle Donnelly created a light, entertaining take on the family with her tale of three sisters in London who turn out to be direct descendants of Jo Bhaer. In 2011, Lauren Baratz-Logsted published *Little Women and Me,* a middle-grade novel about a young girl who becomes so engrossed in Alcott's novel that she's transported into the story, becoming the fifth March sister. "She has identified with Jo and has some of Jo's predilections, but actually finds Jo a little bit annoying and manages to have some of Jo's adventures herself," Clark says of Emily, the book's plucky protagonist.

In her Pulitzer Prize–winning 2005 novel, *March,* Geraldine Brooks retells *Little Women* from the point of view of Mr. March by chronicling his experiences in the Civil War and embellishing the character's story with elements taken from Bronson Alcott's life. "I wouldn't have the hubris to attempt to rewrite Louisa May Alcott, so I've just taken the bit of the story she didn't want to deal with, for whatever complex psychological or Freudian reasons," Brooks said in a 2005 interview with BookPage. "I hope that people who love *Little Women* will see it as a respectful homage to Louisa May."

In her 2017 novel *This Wide Night,*

IN A 1977 EPISODE OF THE series *Little House on the Prairie,* Mary (Melissa Sue Anderson), Ginny (Rachel Longaker), Laura (Mellisa Gilbert), and Nellie (Alison Arngrim) performed in a school play based on *Little Women.*

Sarvat Hasin transposes the tale to 1970s Pakistan and tells it in the voice of the Laurie character. According to Beverly Lyon Clark, the book is only one example of *Little Women*'s continued influence in international circles. "It suggests how *Little Women* has spoken to and in some way still speaks to people around the world," says Clark, a professor of English at Wheaton College in Norton, Massachusetts. "It speaks to both very modern values of feminism and independence for women and also to traditional family values. You could read it either way."

Rey Terciero certainly took a more radical view of Alcott's source material when creating the 2019 graphic novel *Meg, Jo, Beth, and Amy: A Modern Retelling of Little Women* with artist Bre Indigo. They not only wanted to represent characters of color, by having the sisters be a part of a blended family, but also to have Jo come to terms with her sexual orientation at the end of the story. "I grew up as a young gay kid in Texas, and there wasn't any character I could relate to, but there was something in Jo that I remember identifying with," says Terciero. "I was like, I feel like she and I have something in common. It was like a secret. When I wanted to recast it as a modern-day graphic novel, I definitely wanted to have Jo be able to come out. Because 150 years ago, that wasn't really an option for those characters, but now, it is."

Terciero believes it's a testament to Alcott's vision and progressive nature that *Little Women* can exist in so many guises, speaking to so many different audiences in so many varied ways.

"I think back to classic literature like Charles Dickens and Jane Austen. They're stories that still resonate but they don't have the kind of translation that *Little Women* does," Terciero says. "All of Jane Austen's books were about getting married... With *Little Women*, it wasn't just about getting married. It was very much about finding your voice and being a good sister and being supportive of the family. Those are themes that are so important, even today." ●

PHOTO CREDITS

Front Cover: Columbia Pictures/Entertainment Pictures/Alamy **Back Cover:** Everett **Page 1:** Courtesy Louisa May Alcott's Orchard House **Pages 2–3:** Columbia Pictures/Album/Alamy

INTRODUCTION
Page 5: Bridgeman Images **Pages 6–7:** Wilson Webb/Sony Pictures/PictureLux/The Hollywood Archive/Alamy **Pages 8–9:** Courtesy Louisa May Alcott's Orchard House

CHAPTER 1
Pages 10–12: Courtesy Louisa May Alcott's Orchard House (2) **Page 13:** Courtesy Everett Collection/Shutterstock **Pages 14–15** (left to right): Courtesy Concord Free Public Library; Courtesy Louisa May Alcott's Orchard House **Pages 16–17** (clockwise from top): Sarin Images/Granger; Courtesy Louisa May Alcott's Orchard House; Trey Powers Photography/Courtesy Louisa May Alcott's Orchard House **Page 18** (from top): Interim Archives/Archive/Getty; Courtesy Louisa May Alcott's Orchard House **Page 19:** Courtesy Concord Free Public Library **Pages 20–21:** Courtesy Louisa May Alcott's Orchard House (3) **Page 22** (left to right): National Geographic Image Collection/Alamy; Bettmann/Getty **Page 23:** Look and Learn/Bridgeman **Page 24:** Courtesy Louisa May Alcott's Orchard House **Page 25:** Lebrecht Authors/Bridgeman **Page 26** (from top): Courtesy Louisa May Alcott's Orchard House; Granger **Page 27:** Bridgeman **Page 28:** Look and Learn/Bridgeman **Page 29:** Courtesy Louisa May Alcott's Orchard House **Pages 30–31** (left to right): Culture Club/Hulton Archive/Getty (3) **Page 32:** Courtesy Louisa May Alcott's Orchard House **Page 33:** Chronicle/Alamy **Pages 34–35** (left to right): Album/Alamy; Courtesy Louisa May Alcott's Orchard House; Chronicle/Alamy **Pages 36–39:** Courtesy Louisa May Alcott's Orchard House (6)

CHAPTER 2
Pages 40–41: © PBS/BBC/Courtesy Everett **Page 42:** Snap/Shutterstock **Page 43:** RKO/Kobal/Shutterstock **Page 44** (from top): Sportsphoto/Alamy; Courtesy Louisa May Alcott's Orchard House (2) **Page 45:** Ullstein Bild/Getty **Page 46:** Moviestore Collection/Alamy **Page 47:** Courtesy Everett **Pages 48–49** (left to right): Pictorial Parade/Archive Photos/Getty; Courtesy Everett **Pages 50–51:** © Columbia Pictures/Courtesy Everett (2) **Pages 52–53:** © Columbia Pictures, Courtesy Photofest **Page 53:** Joseph Lederer/Di Novi/Columbia/Kobal/Shutterstock **Page 54:** Jody Rogac/The New York Times/Redux **Page 55:** Columbia Pictures/Album/Alamy **Pages 56–57** (left to right): Wilson Webb/Sony Pictures/PictureLux/The Hollywood Archive/Alamy; Lifestyle Pictures/Alamy **Pages 58–59:** Columbia Pictures/Album/Alamy **Pages 60–61** (clockwise from top left): Wilson Webb/Sony Pictures/PictureLux/The Hollywood Archive/Alamy (2); Little Women: The Official Movie Companion Cover © 2019 Columbia Pictures Industries, Inc. All Rights Reserved **Pages 62–63:** Columbia Pictures/Entertainment Pictures/Alamy **Page 64:** Jerry Tavin/Everett **Page 65:** ANL/Shutterstock **Pages 66–67:** Bud Gray/MPTVimages **Pages 68–69:** © PBS/BBC/Courtesy Everett **Pages 70–71:** Joe McNally/Getty **Pages 72–73:** Sara Krulwich/The New York Times/Redux (2)

CHAPTER 3
Pages 74–75: Trey Powers Photography/Courtesy Louisa May Alcott's Orchard House **Pages 76–77:** Andrew O'Brien/Alamy **Pages 78–79:** Herb K. Barnett/Courtesy Louisa May Alcott's Orchard House **Pages 80-81** (clockwise from top left): Herb K. Barnett/Courtesy Louisa May Alcott's Orchard House; Trey Powers Photography/Courtesy Louisa May Alcott's Orchard House (2) **Pages 82–83:** Trey Powers Photography/Courtesy Louisa May Alcott's Orchard House (3) **Page 84:** Trunk Archive **Page 85:** Elliott Erwitt/Magnum **Pages 86–87** (clockwise from top left) Christopher Lane/Contour by Getty; Luciano Viti/Getty; James Estrin/The New York Times/Redux **Pages 88–89** (left to right): Fotosearch/Getty; Stuart Conway/Camera Press/Redux; Stephen Voss/Redux **Page 90:** Kodansha Blue Bird Library/Courtesy Louisa May Alcott's Orchard House **Page 91:** Courtesy Little, Brown Books for Young Readers **Pages 92–93:** NBC **Pages 94–95:** Columbia Pictures/Entertainment Pictures/Alamy **Page 96:** Courtesy Louisa May Alcott's Orchard House

IN 2019'S *LITTLE WOMEN*, THE March sisters put on one of their trademark theatrical performances. Saoirse Ronan's Jo stands behind Emma Watson's Meg, seated, left, and Florence Pugh's Amy.

LINES BY LOUISA

"FAR AWAY THERE IN THE SUNSHINE ARE MY HIGHEST ASPIRATIONS. I MAY NOT REACH THEM, BUT I CAN LOOK UP AND SEE THEIR BEAUTY, BELIEVE IN THEM AND TRY TO FOLLOW WHERE THEY LEAD."

Made in the USA
Middletown, DE
22 September 2020

CLASSIC RENDERING
Three March sisters, Amy (Joan Bennett), Jo (Katharine Hepburn), and Meg (Frances Dee), in 1933's *Little Women*.

ISBN 978-1-5478-5153-9
EAN
9 781547 851539 >